SOCCER

AHEAD·OF·THE·GAME

SOCCER

WARD LOCK

MIKE McGLYNN •

First published in 1990 by Ward Lock

Villiers House, 41–47 Strand,
London WC2N 5TE, England

A Cassell imprint

© Text and illustrations Ward Lock 1990

All rights reserved. No part of this publication may be reproduced or transmitted in any form or by any means, electronic or mechanical including photocopying, recording or any information storage or retrieval system, without prior permission in writing from the publishers.

ISBN 0 7063 6886 X

Text set in 10/11pt Compugraphic Triumvirate
by BP Integraphics, Bath, Avon
Printed and bound in Great Britain
at Richard Clays

The author and publishers would like to thank Colorsport for supplying photographs.

Frontispiece: The importance of getting into line with the ball and selecting the correct controlling surface are very well illustrated by Liverpool's Kenny Dalglish controlling the ball with his chest.

CONTENTS

Introduction *6*

ONE: Ball control *8*
TWO: Defensive play *17*
THREE: Midfield play *31*
FOUR: Attacking play *47*
FIVE: Goalkeeping *65*
SIX: Set plays and re-starts *86*
SEVEN: Fitness training for soccer *102*
EIGHT: Injuries: prevention and cure *119*
NINE: Professional style *121*

Testing Time: Questions *125*
             Answers *127*
Index *128*

INTRODUCTION

Welcome to *Ahead of the Game*. If you bought the first book in the series, *Play the Game*, then you are familiar with the basic skills of Association Football. With *Ahead of the Game* we are now going to develop those skills further and help you to improve your game.

But playing soccer is not just about being able to kick the ball, tackle, take throw ins and so on. A large part of the game revolves around physical fitness – a very important area in all sports these days. And we will advise you how best to develop this side of your game.

They say that practice makes perfect and, believe me, that principle certainly applies to football. The more you practise the better you will become. But don't think practising is boring. It doesn't have to be and we have worked out some routines for you that will both improve your game and, at the same time, be fun to do.

As we look at each aspect of the game, ball control, dribbling, shooting, goalkeeping, and so on, we advise you how to perfect each of the skills and point out potential mistakes. Each discipline is complemented with a training schedule to assist with your advancement.

Soccer is very much a team game, but many exercises can be carried out either on your own or with just one or two teammates. You will soon appreciate how these exercises can be applied to real match situations.

Another area we cover is injuries. With a contact sport like soccer, injuries will inevitably occur. We can advise what to do when you suffer an injury because the wrong action, or no action at all, can have disastrous consequences. Hopefully some of the tips we give you about injury prevention will eliminate, or reduce, your risk of being out of the game for long spells.

No matter what your position, whether it be in goal, in defence, in midfield or as one of your team's strikers, *Ahead of the Game* has something for you and if you read the book and adhere to the training sessions outlined, then it will help to improve your game.

Soccer is a great game to play. The more you play the more you will enjoy it. And the more you play the more you will want to improve. *Ahead of the Game* will play a useful part in your future development.

Mike McGlynn

Liverpool and England player John Barnes shows good balance, control and vision while running with the ball.

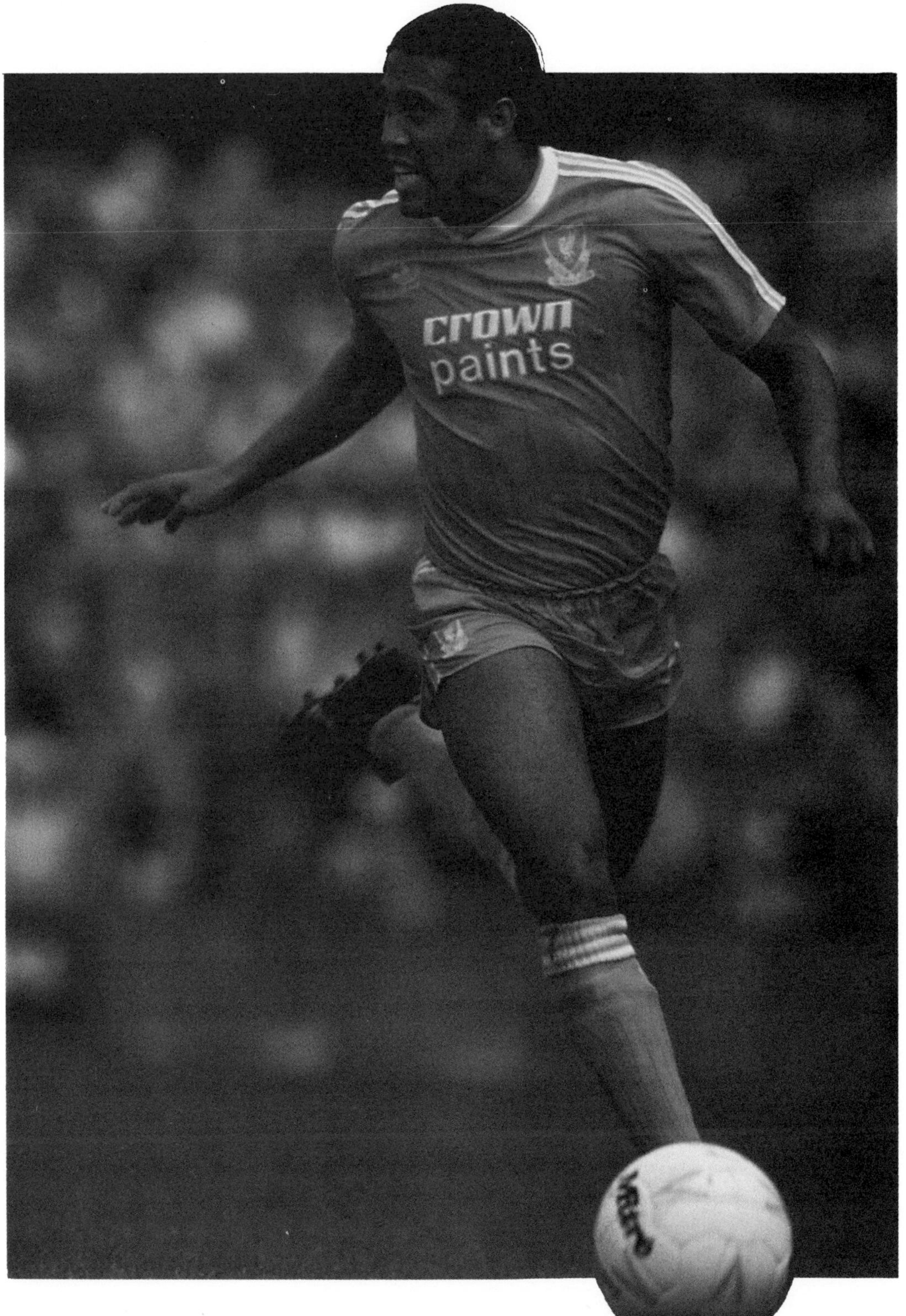
crown
paints

ONE

BALL CONTROL

Throw somebody a football and ask him to control it. Invariably he will stop the ball dead. However, in a match this rarely occurs because control is nothing on its own but is a means to an end. We control the ball to pass, dribble, and shoot.

The word 'control' has been replaced with the word 'touch' in footballing vocabulary in recent years. Touch refers to your first touch of the ball and a good first touch will give you time to assess your next movement accurately.

The confidence which a good first touch can bring will improve all other aspects of your game. Being comfortable and confident on the ball is the most important attribute of all top-class players.

The three areas of the body which you need to develop as areas of control are the feet, thighs and chest. Although heading is dealt with in other chapters, it should be remembered it is also a means of controlling the ball.

There are three key factors you need to observe when controlling the ball:

1 Move into the line of the ball. Don't wait for the ball to come to you: move towards it so your first touch takes you in the direction you want to go.

2 Select the correct controlling part of your body. The way the ball comes to you will dictate which area of your body you use to control the ball. Make sure you select the correct one.

3 Select the correct type of control/touch on the ball. Again it is important that your selection be correct. Your position, and what you want to do next will be major factors in your decision.

There are two forms of control: (i) the soft or cushioned control, and (ii) the firm or wedged control.

With (i) the controlling surface should be relaxed, allowing the pace to be taken off the ball. This type of control is usually used in a tight situation where there is room only to move the ball a few feet (about 1m).

When using (ii) the controlling surface must be firm. You would use this type of control when you have space around you allowing you to move the ball several yards or metres.

Hard work on these three aspects of your game is the springboard for greater success.

We will now look in a little more detail at the three controlling surfaces, starting with the most used, the feet.

BALL · CONTROL

Top players are comfortable on the ball and aware of the movements of their teammates and of the opposition.

Receiving the ball on the instep.

FOOT · CONTROL

Control should be practised using both feet. Top-class players are comfortable and happy to receive the ball with either foot. During a game, you will receive the ball from many different angles; so it's important to practise using all parts of the foot – inside, outside and the instep.

The following practice sessions can be carried out either on your own, using a wall as a rebounding surface, or with a playing partner in a 10yd (9m) square.

SOCCER

Ball control.
Simple sidefoot passing.
(Approx 10 yds square)
Using a wall as a rebound surface for control practice.

Session one – ground control

Players should try to control with their first touch and return the pass with their second. The techniques to be practised are:

Inside of the foot
(a) Control the ball with the inside of either foot.
(b) Play the ball slightly away from your feet.
(c) With your next touch, return the pass with the inside of the same foot.
    You can develop the exercise as follows:
(a) Control the ball with the inside of your right foot.
(b) Play the ball across your body.
(c) With your next touch, return the pass with the inside of your left foot.
    A further development would be:
(a) Control the ball with the inside of either foot.
(b) Play the ball slightly in front of you.
(c) With your next touch, return the pass with the outside of the same foot.

Outside of the foot
(a) Control the ball with the outside of either foot.
(b) Play the ball slightly in front of you.
(c) With your next touch, return the pass with the outside of the same foot.
    You can develop the exercise as follows:
(a) Control the ball with the outside of the foot.
(b) Move the ball slightly to one side.
(c) With your next touch return the pass with the inside of the same foot.

The instep
(a) Control the ball and return the pass using the instep of the same foot.
(b) Control the ball with the instep, return the pass with the inside of the same foot.

BALL · CONTROL

Ball control.

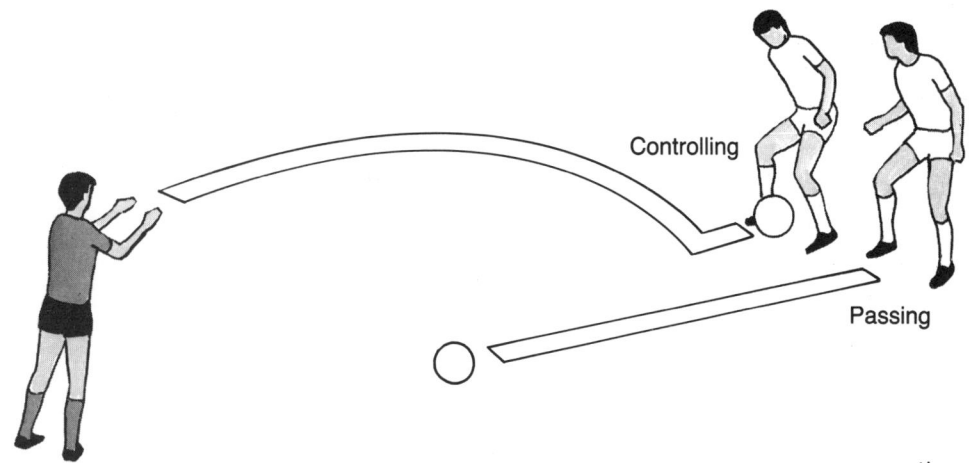

(c) Control the ball with the instep, return the pass with the outside of the same foot.

Session two – control from balls in the air

All practices from session one can be repeated for session two.
  You can develop the exercises as follows:
(a) With your first touch, move the ball into the corner of the grid.
(b) Play the ball back to your partner with the second touch.
  The next stage is to put the practice sessions to the real test by trying them under pressure.

Session three – playing under pressure

(a) Y plays the ball to X
(b) Y follows the ball, putting pressure on X.
(c) X has to control the ball away from the oncoming Y in order to play a pass through the goal.

Practice routine for Session Three.

SOCCER

A two against one formation, Session Four.

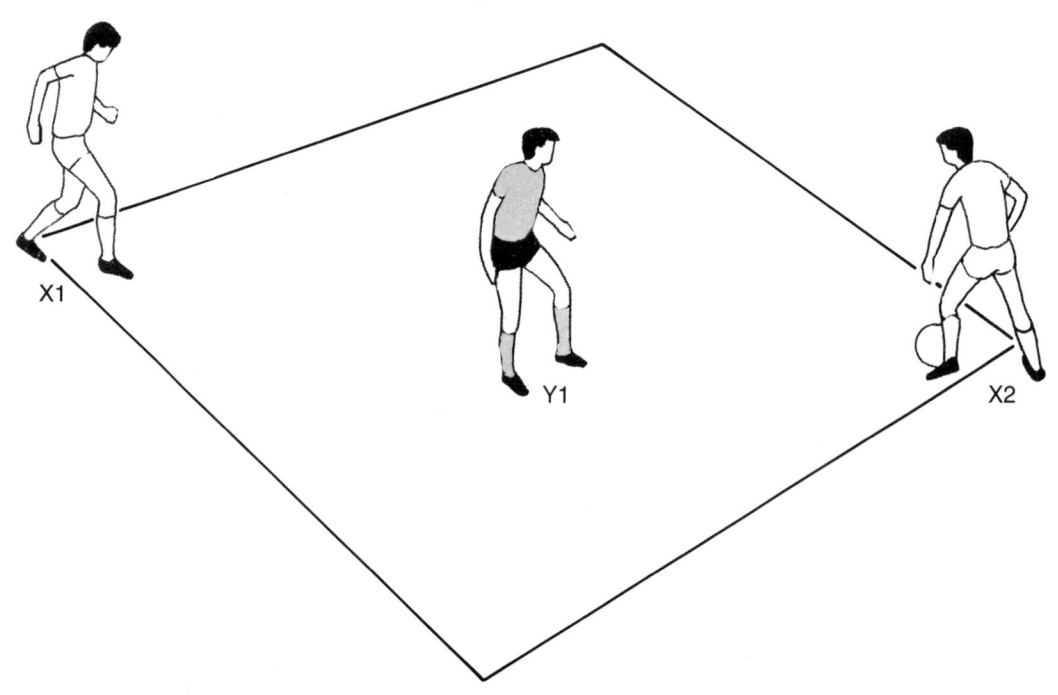

Session four – two against one

(a) X1 and X2 have to keep possession from Y.
(b) X1 and X2 are allowed only two touches; one to control the ball, and one to pass.
(c) To practise the quality of the first touch, the ball should be played away from the defender into space. The receiving player should take time to look up, assess the position of his partner, and play a correctly weighted pass.

THIGH · CONTROL

The thigh is not used as much as it might be in top-class football, and its use should be practised.

The two biggest problems of controlling the ball with the thighs are that it often hits the knee instead, and that the thigh is moving upwards when it comes into contact with the ball. In both cases the ball usually bounces up, off and away from you.

BALL · CONTROL

Controlling the ball with the thigh.

Controlling the ball with the chest.

SOCCER

Always control the ball with the middle part of the thigh, which should be relaxed on contact with the ball. At the point of contact, your leg should be moving downwards, which will allow the ball to drop just in front of you. This technique can be practised by yourself; throw the ball above your head and control it with your thigh.

As with control with the feet, you can deflect the ball to one side, thus allowing a confident and accurate second touch.

The same practice sessions for controlling the ball with the feet can be used for improving technique with the thigh.

CHEST · CONTROL

The chest provides us with the body's largest controlling surface, but when opportunities arise in the game to use it, many players usually try something else.

One of the main reasons for this is fear of making a mistake – because of a lack of confidence, and because they think a ball controlled on the chest will hurt on impact. It won't if carried out correctly.

Body position is important; your arms should spread out slightly from your side giving you good balance and an open chest area.

The point of impact is important. Many players tense up when they see a ball coming towards their chest. Consequently the controlling surface becomes solid and the ball rebounds away.

As the ball comes into contact with your chest, relax the contact area. This will create a hollow, allowing the ball to drop to your feet. Breathing out as the ball arrives will create the necessary hollow.

England's Neil Webb assesses 'what's on' before delivering a 'lofted pass' forward.

BALL · CONTROL

SOCCER

Bending your head and shoulders slightly forward will help to guide the ball down from your chest to your feet.

The aim is to get the ball to your feet as quickly as possible. But, as in our other practice sessions there are times when this will not be possible and you will need to deflect the ball away.

On these occasions thrust your chest forward, this time creating the firm rebound service, and deflect the ball in whichever direction you choose a couple of feet away from the player marking you.

Session one

Get a team-mate to throw a ball to you. Control it with your chest and pass the ball back to him.

As you improve, try to perform the technique with two touches.

To create a game situation, after your partner has served the ball to you, get him to move towards you and put pressure on you. Try getting the ball to your feet quickly enough to allow you to dribble past him as he attacks you. Alternatively, use a firm chest to play the ball past him as he moves towards you, then collect the ball and with your second touch shoot for goal.

A good illustration to show the need for perfect control is when a player is receiving the ball with his back to his opponent's goal. Forwards often find themselves in this situation, closely marked by a defender on the edge of the penalty area. Top strikers like Ian Rush and Mark Hughes are examples of players who have the ability to control the ball well in such a situation and create an attacking movement. The speed and quality of their first touch creates vital shooting opportunities. To help you develop similar skills, try the following practice, first without a defender then, as you get better, with a defender marking you.

Get the person making the pass to you to vary the pace of the ball, and to play balls on which you can use the three controlling areas of your body. Your choice of controlling surface and the speed at which you make that decision are vital, so this is an excellent practice.

Don't forget that you must move the ball into a position where the defender cannot get it, making it easier for you to shoot after your first touch. This is an enjoyable practice, with the added incentive of being able to score goals as well as improve your controlling techniques.

The importance of good control and the quality of the first touch mark the difference between a good player and a top-class one. Watch the top players, especially those who are happy to receive the ball whatever the situation or their position on the pitch. Being comfortable on the ball breeds confidence in all aspects of your play. A sure first touch and subsequent control are two of the basic ingredients for greater success.

TWO

DEFENSIVE PLAY

One of the most exciting aspects of football is the scoring of goals. Many years ago the emphasis was to out-score your opponents and it was not unusual for games to finish 5-4 or 6-5. It would be fair to say that today's game is as much about preventing your opponents from scoring and you are more likely to see games finishing 1-0 or 0-0.

So, these days the role of defender is simple: all you have to do is stop your opponents from scoring. It sounds easy. But top defenders will tell you it isn't.

As an individual, you have to understand how, where and when to defend. You need to develop physical qualities which will help you compete and tackle for the ball, and mental qualities of concentration, patience and self-discipline. These qualities need to be combined with fellow defenders to form a tight-knit unit.

DEFENSIVE · SYSTEMS

All teams play to a defensive system. Most British clubs favour the zonal system in which defenders guard a specific area of the pitch and mark any attacker who enters it. In other parts of the world, teams usually adopt a man-to-man system whereby defenders are assigned to mark one particular player throughout the game. Teams using this system often use a sweeper – a player positioned behind the other defenders, supporting and covering them. Although most teams adopt a specific system it's not uncommon to see teams combining different aspects of each.

SOCCER

Interception practice.

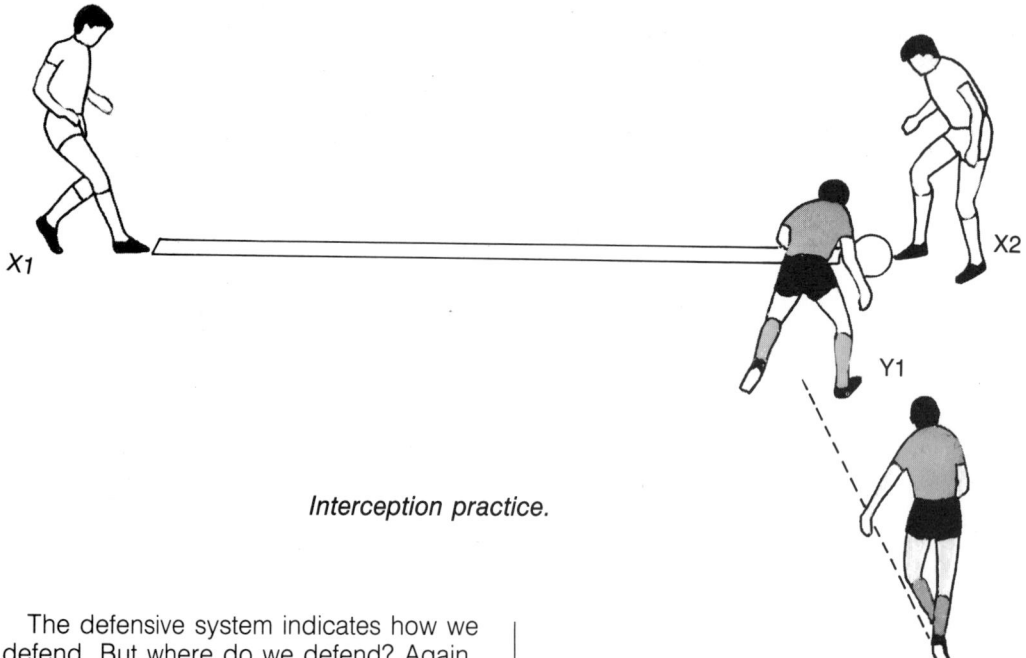

The defensive system indicates how we defend. But where do we defend? Again this is a matter of choice. Some teams will retreat deep into their own half, getting men behind the ball, before confronting their opponents. Others will pressurize as soon as they lose possession, attempting to win the ball back in the same area in which it was lost.

If the 'how' and 'where' of defending is a matter of choice, the 'when' is not open for discussion. You defend as soon as your team loses possession, no matter which part of the pitch it happens on.

Having looked at the defender's role in the overall team pattern, it is important that he has good individual qualities to complement the system. One of the main attributes of a good defender is the ability to win the ball, so he has to be a good hard tackler.

While this is important, it's not always the sole attribute of a good defender. Top defenders such as Bobby Moore and Franz Beckenbauer relied on speed and anticipation which allowed them to intercept passes or 'steal' balls as the attacker was making his first touch. Of the present-day players Liverpool skipper Alan Hansen is an excellent exponent of this technique.

The first thought of a defender should be 'can I intercept?'. The practice illustrated in the diagram above is ideal for developing interception skills.

Defender Y1 has to move as soon as X1 releases the ball. If you are Y1, cover the ground quickly and be confident you can win the ball. If there is any doubt in your mind then you shouldn't be attempting to intercept. That said, hesitation is fatal to the chances of an interception being successful – once you've decided to intercept, move in quickly.

The opportunity to intercept in a game is so brief that often it is missed and the attacker has turned and is facing the defender. Obviously this position poses different problems for the defender.

DEFENSIVE · PLAY

TACKLING

Although you may have decided you cannot intercept it's still important to get as close to the attacker as you can while the ball is travelling to him. While it is important you cover the ground quickly, the run should not be a reckless one. If you rush in too quickly you will be selling yourself and the attacker will be able to knock the ball past you with ease.

When the attacker is about to make his first touch, you, the defender, must put the brakes on, whatever your distance from him. At this point it is important to consider your body position and stance. Your body should be between the ball and the main route to the goal. Your stance should be side on to the attacker, similar to the stance of a fencer, slightly crouched, knees bent. Use your arms for balance and keep your eye on the ball.

It is now a battle of wits between you and the attacker. You must try and manoeuvre him into areas which are least dangerous to your team, *i.e.* towards touchlines, or to force him to play a negative pass, square or backwards. Mental attitude, concentration and patience are vital. But you must not forget your sole aim: to win the ball, which requires a determined and aggressive approach.

In a sense, it is the tackling situation which is at the heart of football, pitting one player's skills against another. In the course of a match, the battle is as much psychological as physical. The early exchanges are particularly important. Swift decisive tackling can dent the confidence of an attacking side and disrupt the pattern of play. On the following pages, we look at the basic tackling techniques.

An example of the block tackle.

SOCCER

The block tackle.
Area: 10 yd (9 m) × 30 yd (27 m)
X1 plays ball to X2.
Y1 has to prevent X1 getting the ball to Y2.

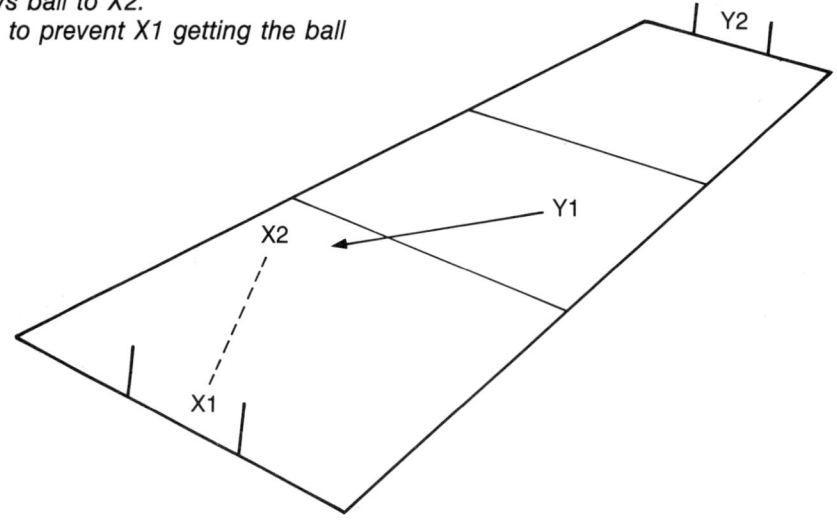

The block tackle

The moment you feel that you can win the ball is the time to tackle, either by getting the ball away from the attacker with your leading foot, or by making a block tackle. The correct body stance is very important in making this tackle and will give you a big advantage and greater chance of winning the ball. A compact body shape is important, enabling you to transfer your weight behind the tackling foot at the moment of the tackle.

Try the same practice as for the interception, but this time the distances between the players now allow the attacker to face the defender.

The other common defending position is when the attacker has his back to your goal. Again your first thought should be to intercept, but failing this you should not allow him to turn. Adopt a low body position ensuring you can see the ball. Your distance from the attacker is vital.

Too close and he could be past you with a quick trick or dummy. Too far away and he can turn and face you. Ideally you want to be just over an arm's length away from the attacker. If you watch top class defenders many will put their hand out in front of them. This is good for balance and is a guide for distance.

With the attacker in this position you, as a defender, have the advantage. Once more, concentration and patience are essential. When the forward decides to turn, make your tackle. As the attacker is half turned, you have to move quickly to either knock the ball away or make a solid tackle. Whatever the choice, the ball has been cleared from a potential danger area.

Remember to be patient in this position. It is very easy to foul the attacker, and a free kick in and around the penalty area can pose a bigger problem. Keep him facing his own goal and be ready to strike the moment he attempts to turn.

DEFENSIVE · PLAY

A defender's body position when attacker is facing him.

Area: 10 yd (9 m) × 30 yd (27 m)
X1 plays the ball to X2 who approaches the ball to collect. Y1 has to close down, maintaining correct distances and to prevent X2 passing the ball to Y2.

SOCCER

DEFENSIVE · PLAY

The sliding tackle

Up to now we have concentrated on stopping your opponents getting past you, but that's not always possible and there are going to be occasions where you will be chasing or running alongside the attacker.

When this occurs you are often forced to make a tackle from the side, usually a sliding tackle.

This is an appropriate time to emphasize one of the golden rules of defending: stay on your feet whenever possible. The minute you fall to the

(Above and Right) Tackling an attacker with his back to goal.

Celtic's Paul McStay, seen here making a sliding tackle.

SOCCER

ground you are effectively out of the game, and your team is down to ten men. Therefore, it is important to understand that when you use the sliding tackle, you must be positive and confident that you can win the ball.

There is no better feeling in football, from an attacker's point of view, than skipping past a hapless full-back left lying on the ground. Don't be that hapless full-back.

The timing of the sliding tackle is critical. Be sure you can make contact with the ball, which will usually be with the foot furthest from the ball. The non tackling leg will act as pivot and will give the tackle strength and support if you go down onto its knee. From this position you can wrap your leg around the ball and win it, or deflect it away.

Some players forced to tackle back use the nearest leg to make the tackle. On these occasions the defender slides towards the ball in the same direction the forward is running, and using the inside leg deflects the ball away or pulls the ball inwards. Watch England's Peter Beardsley, a fine exponent of this tackling technique. Again timing is so important and it's important that once you've made the tackle you get to your feet as quickly as possible.

Another occasion when you would use the sliding tackle would be if the winger had gone past you, was at the dead ball line and was about to cross the ball. The technique is the same, but your priority is to block the cross.

The slide tackle.

DEFENSIVE · PLAY

COVERING

So far we have looked at the techniques of the defender pressurizing the player on the ball. It is also important that he is aware of his duties as a covering defender. Once the first defender has set himself in front of an attacker, the covering player must take up the correct angle and distance of support.

The covering player should not be too far away from the first defender. If he is, the attacker may be able to dribble past the first defender, retain possession and attack the covering player.

It could also prove disastrous if the covering defender is too close to the first defender. A ball can then be played past both of them in one movement, taking the two players out of the game.

The angle of cover will in the first instance depend very much on the angle and body position of the first defender, who also needs to be aware of the position of other attacking players.

To help you appreciate the angles and distances try the following practice:

2 v 1 defence

In this illustration the pressurizing defender X1 has closed down the attacker Y2. His angle of approach is forcing the attacker down the line, and the covering defender X2 is in a position to cover the ground quickly and possibly win the ball should it be knocked down the line. Also, should the attacker Y2 choose to come inside, the covering defender is again well placed for winning the ball.

Communication between defenders is vital. The covering defenders should help the pressurizing player by giving him information such as 'show him the line', 'push him inside' or even advising when it is best for the first defender to make the first tackle.

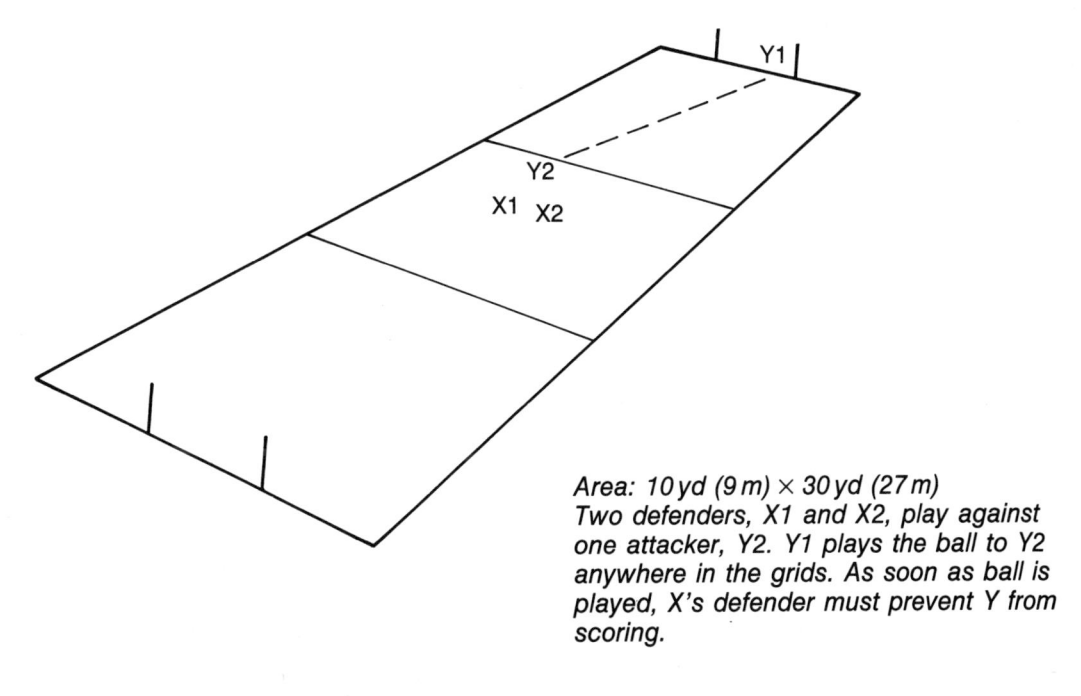

*Area: 10 yd (9 m) × 30 yd (27 m)
Two defenders, X1 and X2, play against one attacker, Y2. Y1 plays the ball to Y2 anywhere in the grids. As soon as ball is played, X's defender must prevent Y from scoring.*

SOCCER

In this 2 v 1 situation in favour of the defender it's easy for the covering defender to judge his distance and angles of support. However, the presence of another attacker will affect his thinking.

An example of this is shown in the following practice:

Developing awareness

You can see from this illustration that defender X2 has to consider the position of the player on the ball, as well as that of attacker Y1. It would be to his advantage if Y2 came inside, so he must convey that information to X1. Encouraging Y2 to come inside would give him the opportunity to make a tackle, or interception should Y2 elect to pass.

This is a good exercise which develops the defenders' awareness of covering positions, distances and angles of support. It quickens reactions and speed of thought. If Y2 gets the ball to Y1 the defending roles are reversed with X2 becoming the pressurizing player and X1 the covering player. Player X1 then has to make quick adjustments with regard to his angles and distances from X2 and the attacking Y's.

What we have looked at so far are the basic foundations of good defending. As an individual you need to understand that the same principles will apply when you move into a game.

To help the gradual learning process of successful defending, try playing a game of 3 v 3 with one goalkeeper per team.

Defenders should remember their individual roles if they are the pressurizing players: stopping the attacker from turning and forcing him a particular way. Covering players should take their line from the pressurizing player, ensuring that distances and angles are right.

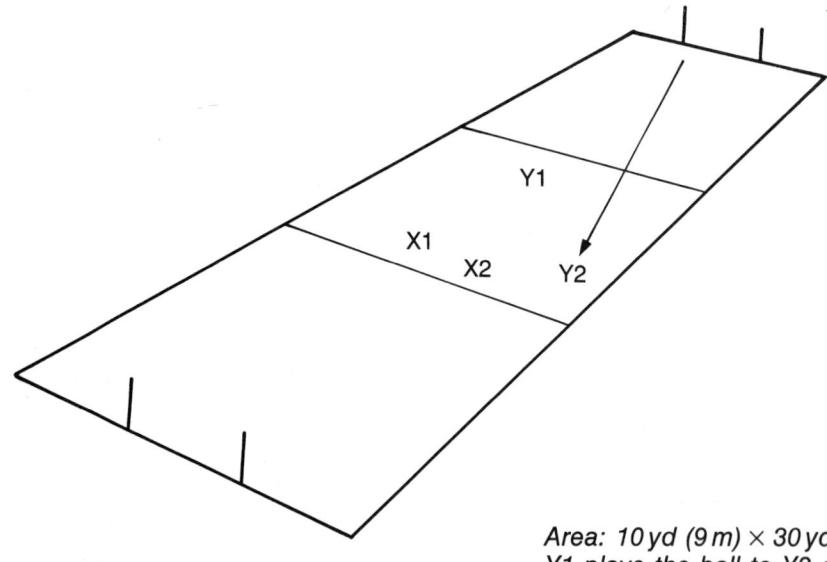

Area: 10 yd (9 m) × 30 yd (27 m)
Y1 plays the ball to Y2 and joins in the play. X1 and X2 have to defend, preventing the Y's from scoring.

DEFENSIVE · PLAY

Heading practice.

HEADING

While a large part of the defender's game involves tackling and work on the ground, there will be many occasions when you will have to defend against a ball in the air. Once again you must understand you are defending and that will determine how you head the ball.

You should try and meet three

Practising the requirements when making a defensive header: achieving height.

1. Aim to head the ball as high as possible. While the ball is in the air your opponents can't score and it gives you and your fellow defenders time to adjust and attack the ball when it comes down.
2. Get distance with your header. In

SOCCER

DEFENSIVE · PLAY

other words, get the ball as far away from your goal as possible. Again this will give you time to adjust and reduce the chances of a quick and successful strike on your goal.

3. Try to head the ball towards the touchlines. This is particularly important if the header you are making is from the centre of your penalty area. As with the other requirements it gives defenders time, since a ball landing in these areas is not an immediate threat on your goal.

To achieve any or all of the above you need to understand the technique. Your first priority is to attack the ball, this will give you momentum to get height and power. Keep your eyes on the ball and contact should be squarely on the forehead. Make sure you head through the bottom half of the ball, so it will travel upwards. Just before contact, arch your back and on contact thrust your neck and shoulders forward, providing power to enable you to head further.

Timing the jump and contact with the ball is crucial for a headed clearance, and you must practise.

Start very simply by throwing a ball up in the air and heading it as far as possible, concentrating on making a correct contact. Then get your partner to throw the ball in the air so you can attack the ball. Concentrate on your timing, which will determine the type of contact with the ball. It is very rarely in a game that you make a header without somebody competing with you, so try your heading exercises with a piggy-in-the-middle.

England's Gary Lineker shows all the required qualities when scoring with this diving header.

SOCCER

Position after a forceful header.

The centre player Y throws the ball to X1 who must head the ball over him to X2. The centre player can jump up and catch or block the header. As you get more proficient the outside players can move further apart.

What we have discussed in this chapter are the basic elements of defending which you need to understand as an individual. Once this is achieved you can go on to combine skills and understanding with your fellow defenders to form a confident defensive unit which in turn will fit into the overall defensive strategy of your team.

THREE

MIDFIELD PLAY

In today's game, midfield is one of the most important positions in the team. The demands and responsibilities are numerous and players have to be aware of all aspects of the game.

The midfield players are the hub of the team; they are the 'engine room', one minute defending in their own penalty area, and the next trying to score goals at the opposite end of the field. As well as defending and attacking, the midfielder has to be able to create openings and convert defence into attack. It would be fair to say that the midfielder's first job is as a defender, supporting his defence and winning the ball.

Having won the ball he takes on the role of creator, switching the team's position from defence to attack. Once the ball is with the forward players, he has to move upfield and support them and, if possible, score himself.

To play in midfield you need plenty of stamina. Combine that with good control and vision, the ability to tackle and pass and, of course, the added bonus of the ability to score goals, and you have the complete midfielder. Watch England captain Bryan Robson in action; he is an excellent example of the all-round skills that are demanded of all midfield players.

It is also helpful to youngsters, if you intend to play in midfield, to play in other positions, such as a full-back or a forward. This will give you an appreciation of the other roles and help your development as an all-round midfield player.

Because the attacking and defensive aspects of the midfield game have been covered in other chapters, we will focus our attention on the creative side of the midfielder's game.

As defending is the first priority of a midfield player, we can assume that on a lot of occasions you are going to win, or receive, the ball in an area somewhere between the edge of your own penalty box and the halfway line. This area will act as a springboard for your team's attack. Sure positional play and control of this area of the field are the basis of many winning teams.

Creative midfield play can usually be achieved in one of two ways: you can pass the ball or you can run with it, which may result in a pass or shot at goal. It may also require you to dribble or go past a defender.

First let's look at running with the ball – a feature of the English game which is not encouraged enough, but one which shows individual skills at their best, and which can dramatically change the run of play.

SOCCER

RUNNING · WITH · THE · BALL

The value of running with the ball can be appreciated by watching the national sides of Holland, Sweden and Denmark, whose players take every opportunity to run with the ball, committing defenders and creating openings for themselves and their team-mates. Many players will say that running with the ball is something you do naturally but like other techniques it needs to be practised.

When practising running with the ball you should remember the following two basic principles:

(a) Cover the ground as quickly as possible.
(b) Make as few touches of the ball as possible.

The beauty of practising running with the ball is you can do it on your own. All you need is a ball. Make sure the ball stays in front of you and does not get stuck between your feet. This problem can be avoided if you use the instep of your boot to move the ball forward. The ball should always be played with the leading foot in the course of your natural stride pattern.

Start practising slowly until you feel comfortable with the technique. As you move faster, you will notice that you are taking fewer touches. At this stage it is worth remembering to practise with both feet; try alternating your leading foot on a set run. In both cases, your stride pattern should be smooth and unbroken, with the

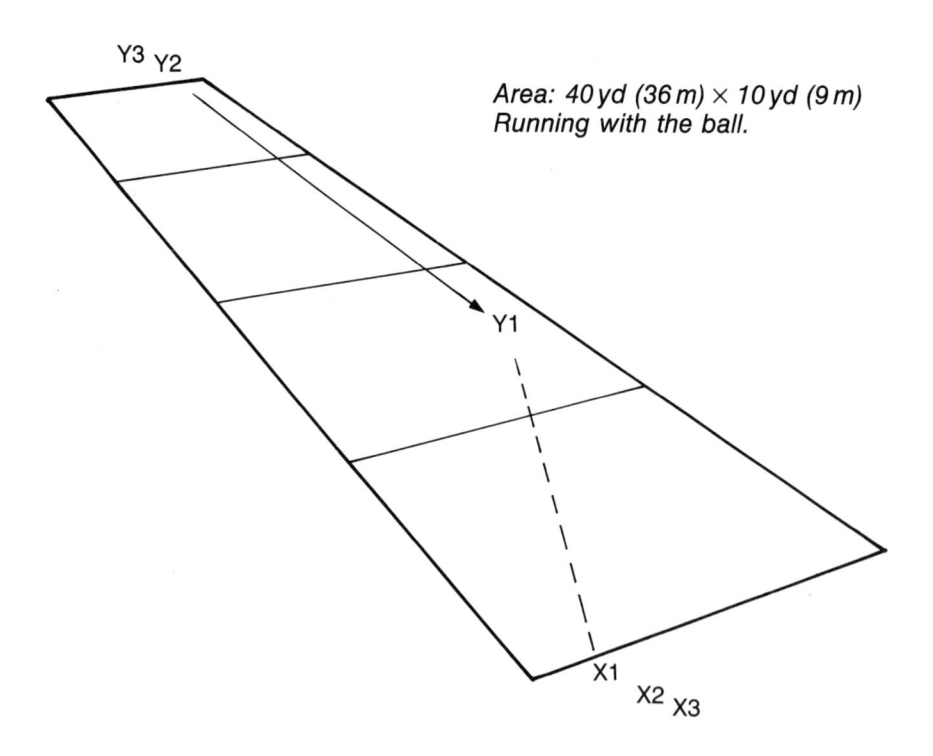

*Area: 40 yd (36 m) × 10 yd (9 m)
Running with the ball.*

MIDFIELD · PLAY

ball coaxed or pushed with the leading foot.

When you play the ball forward remember the one golden rule; keep it within playing distance. This, of course, will depend on the proximity of your nearest opponent. The further away he is, the further you can play the ball in front of you; the closer he is, the closer you keep the ball to you.

Being aware of opponent(s) and what is happening in front of you requires awareness. Once you are comfortable and confident moving the ball, it is time for you to move with the ball at your feet and at the same time get your head up to assess your position. Do this when you have played the ball forward. A quick look up then will tell you what to do next. You may be near an opponent with a team-mate nearby to pass to, or you may have an opportunity to take a shot at goal. Only by quickly looking up can you assess the alternatives available to you.

So when practising, you now want to start lifting your head as you run with the ball. But, again, start slowly at first and as you gain more confidence increase your speed.

This may appear simple, but being confident and comfortable when running with the ball are two of the key elements of a good midfielder.

We can now look at developing these techniques into practices similar to match situations.

Receiving passes

This practice starts with Y1 running with the ball and playing a pass to X1, who repeats the movement taking the ball up to Y2 and so on. It is a form of relay race using a football instead of a baton.

When you are receiving the pass you should be on your toes and ready to move quickly, not waiting back on your heels. Move towards the ball as it comes to you and with a firm touch, play it into the space you are going to move into.

Your movement towards the ball is the first stride of your run. Provided your touch is good, you are off and running and gaining valuable time for your team. This exercise is a simulation of a situation which occurs regularly during a match.

Making passes

Remembering the points about running with the ball, now make the pass. Having encouraged you to move the ball with your leading foot we will now show you how to make the pass with the same foot. Being able to play the ball with your leading foot will keep your movement fluent and help you to gain valuable time because you don't need to make body adjustments, or even stop to play the ball. If you watch England's Chris Waddle you will see that he frequently does this. The ball can be played with the front of the foot, the instep, or with the outside of the foot. The latter enables a swerve to be put on the ball.

Return to the previous exercise, but this time the player(s) receiving the ball should move along the base line. This way, the player with the ball will have to look up to see where the intended receiver has moved to before making the pass. This helps to develop the technique and improves the quality of the pass.

Awareness of space and, more importantly, being ready to attack that area, should be uppermost in the mind of the player receiving the ball. To help develop this, the player running with the ball in the exercise should play the ball once he has entered the third grid. When he has played the ball he should follow the line of the ball thus putting pressure on the player receiving it.

As the ball is coming to him, the receiver should decide where the free area is away from the incoming player. He

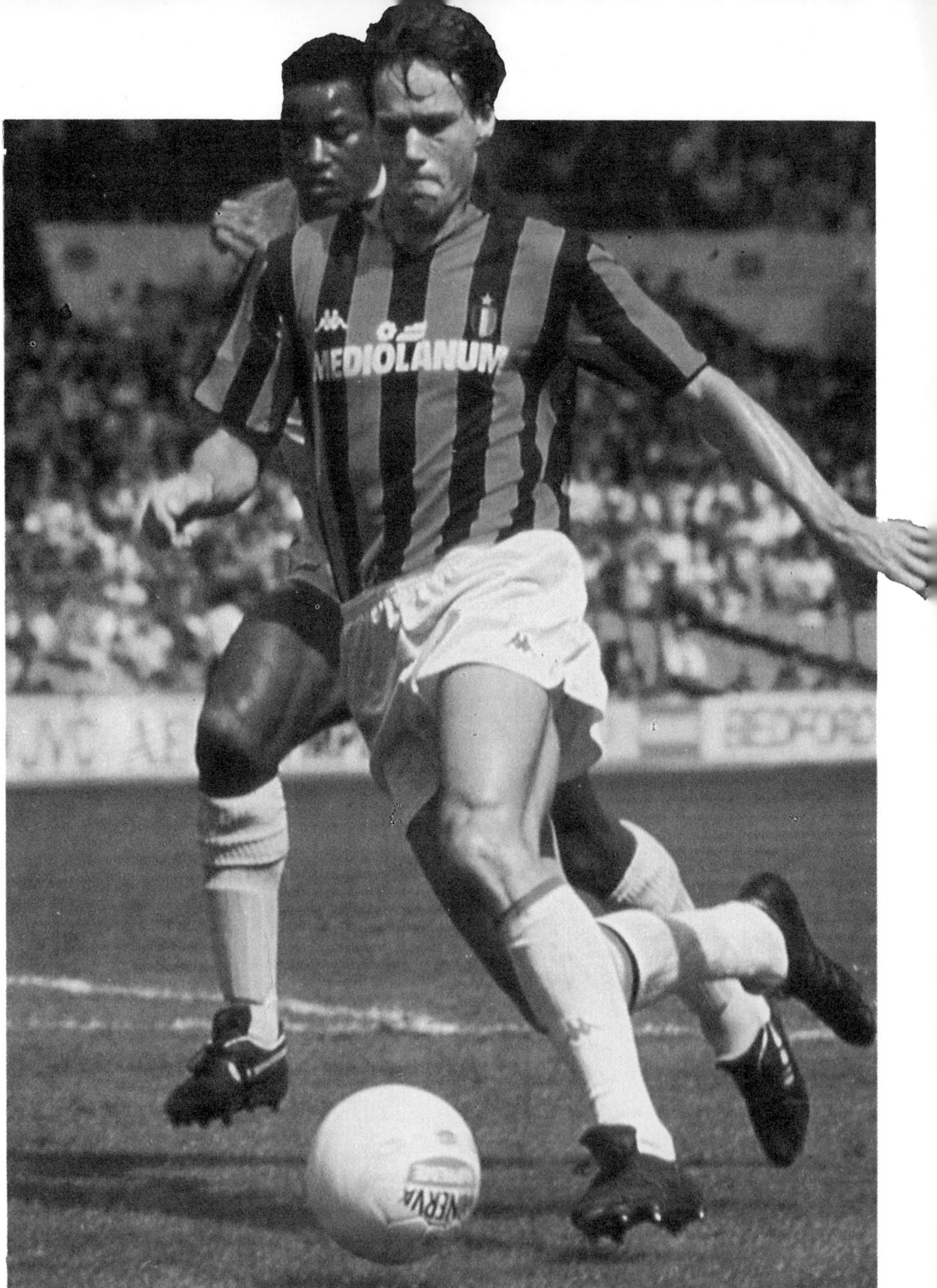
MEDIOLANUM

MIDFIELD · PLAY

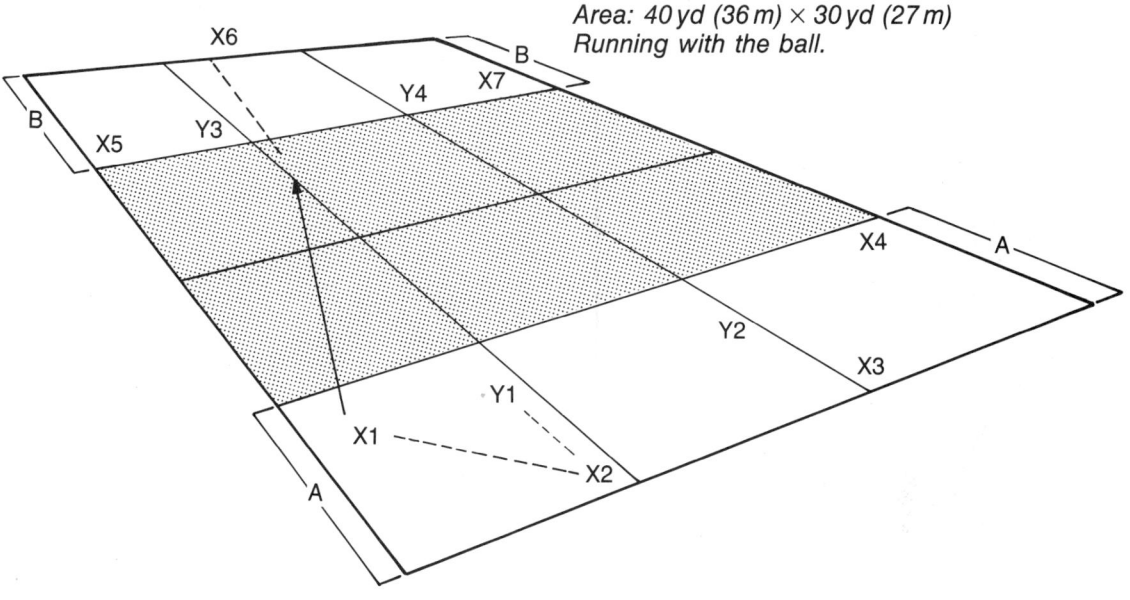

*Area: 40 yd (36 m) × 30 yd (27 m)
Running with the ball.*

Defender Y1 plays the ball to any of the Xs. The Xs combine passes but at the earliest opportunity must run the ball out of the bottom area (A–A), cross the shaded area and deliver a pass to one of the Xs in area (B–B).

In the position illustrated, X1 will remain in area (B–B) creating the same 4 v 2 situation which started the practice. Again the Xs combine but must look to run the ball out at the earliest opportunity. Only the player with the ball is allowed in the shaded area.

should move on to the ball and attack the area he has decided to move into. This is typical of match situations and should be practised regularly. To help make it more realistic and more difficult, the player passing the ball should make the pass at differing angles.

Holland's Marco Van Basten, one of Europe's leading goal-scorers, quick on the turn and an excellent striker of the ball.

Developing awareness

The final practice, shown in the illustration, will help improve your running with the ball and will teach you how your body position will help develop your awareness of what space is available.

Players waiting to receive the ball should, wherever possible, adopt a side-on position where you are able to see both the ball and what is in front of you. Where space is available, you should run the ball into it, then cover the ground as quickly as possible, remembering the quality of the pass is just as important as the run.

SOCCER

Like all aspects of football, confidence plays an important part in running with the ball. So having seen the space, go for it. Be strong, be confident, and don't forget the quality of your shot, cross or pass at the end of it. Many a good run is spoilt with poor finishing.

DRIBBLING

As is often the case in a game, you will not run very far before you are confronted by a defender. You then have to make a decision: Do I pass or do I try and dribble past him? The movements of other players on the pitch will play an important part in that decision. But equally important is the mental attitude of the player with the ball at his feet. Doubts, or lack of confidence in the ability to take on and beat a defender, will result in a pass being made but players like John Barnes and Chris Waddle relish the opportunity to take on an opponent.

It is important that you understand the key elements of dribbling and go on to develop and practise the techniques.

Because of the close proximity of the defender you will require closer ball control. You then have to try and get him to move and get past him. There are several ways of doing this. You can sell him the dummy by tricking him into believing you are going one way, when you really intend to go the other. Another way of getting past the defender is by rapidly changing your pace. The run by Maradona against England during their game in the 1986 World Cup finals, when scoring Argentina's second goal, is an excellent example of these elements being combined in one run.

Some players use the same method or 'trick' for beating a player while others will be guided by the situation they are in. Watching Maradona, Barnes and Waddle will do you no harm and will help you build up your own repertoire of dribbling movements.

Having good close control is the most important first stage of being a good dribbler. The simplest exercise to practise it is to dribble the ball in and out of a line of objects in a slalom manner.

As with running with the ball, start off slowly and concentrate on not hitting the objects or over-running the ball. Use the inside and outside of the foot as you weave between the objects, again practise with both feet alternating each as the leading foot. As you get better, go faster through the course.

Your approach towards the defender should be at a moderate speed. This, with close control, allows you to lift your head and see what is 'on' beyond the defender.

Once you have decided what you are going to do next, you are in a position to commit the defender. It could be with a sudden change in pace, in which case you will simply knock the ball past him.

MIDFIELD · PLAY

Being confident, your speed will help get you to the ball before he has chance to regain his ground. You can also commit the defender by unbalancing or wrong-footing him, which is usually achieved with a trick or feint making him believe you are going one way when you are in fact going another.

The feint

The most common and easiest method of wrong-footing a defender is the feint, and you should practise it first on your own, and when you feel confident practise with some team-mates as 'opposition'.

In the example, imagine the cone to be a defender. Move towards it with the ball and when you are approximately 3ft. (1m) away go into the following routine:

(a) With the inside of your right foot move the ball to your left side, bend your left knee and lean your upper body to the left.

(b) Quickly get the outside of your right foot behind the ball.

(c) With the right foot push the ball past the cone and accelerate.

As with all practice exercises, start off slowly, even at walking pace if necessary. Only as you improve and feel more confident should you increase the pace.

Practise 'beating the man moves' on your own against a cone.

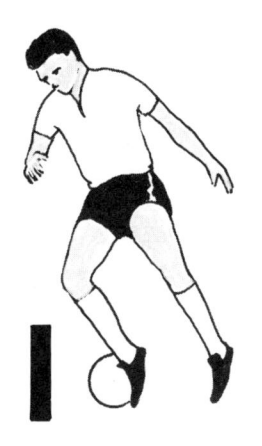

SOCCER

The feint in action.

The scissors

Using the cone(s) again, we will look at an example of a trick known as 'the scissors'.

(a) Play the ball slightly to the right of you with the instep.
(b) Look as though you are going to play the ball with the outside of your right foot, but then step over the ball.
(c) With the ball slightly underneath you, push the ball away with the outside of your left foot.

Once again, start off slowly until you feel comfortable. It will help both techniques if you adopt a low body position, so remember to bend your knees.

We can now put our techniques to the test by trying them in a practice situation.

The important thing to remember now is that once the 'trick' or feint has been performed you must get past the defender with pace. Unless he falls over, the defender will be put off balance only for a fraction of a second, so you must take full advantage and once you get past him you must be strong, determined, and make sure you achieve your next goal, whether it be a pass, cross, or shot.

The scissors is just one example of a trick. Watch the top class players and see how they beat their opponents. Copy them and practise their techniques. The more equipped you are, the more confident you will be as a player. Finally, remember that dribbling is a matter of percentages and even the best dribblers are usually likely to fail more often than they succeed.

MIDFIELD · PLAY

The 'scissors' is a valuable trick when perfected.

SOCCER

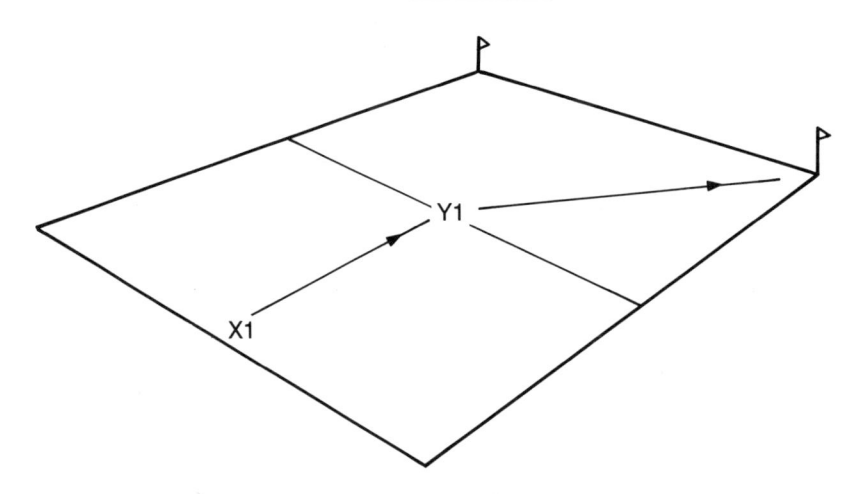

Y1 plays the ball to X1 who is back on the base line, who then advances and tries to commit and beat Y1 with a trick or feint, and get the ball to one of the corners before Y1 has a chance to recover.

PASSING

The other option open to the midfield player if he can't run with the ball is to pass. Once again we need to look at the type and quality of the pass.

The purpose of the pass is generally to switch play from defence to attack as quickly as possible. It is unlikely that a ball passed 5–6ft (1.5–2m) will do this. The pass we will be looking at in detail is the one of between 20 and 30yd (18 and 27m).

Passing is not just a case of booting the ball upfield and hoping one of your team-mates collects it. It has to be delivered with quality and accuracy. Let us now look at passing techniques.

The lofted pass

This pass goes over the defenders' heads and into open space behind. This is the sort of pass attackers like Ian Rush and Gary Lineker thrive on.

As you receive the ball, with a good firm touch, play the ball out of your feet. Your approach should be at a slight angle and your non-kicking foot should be in a comfortable position at the side of the ball. Your body position is very important when passing. Your upper body should be leaning slightly backwards and your head should be kept steady with your eyes looking at the ball.

Contact should be with the instep through the bottom half of the ball. Once you have kicked the ball, allow your foot to follow through the kicking action. This will help with the quality and accuracy of the pass. So, three key points to remember about passing are approach, body position, and contact.

Having looked at the technique we can now put it into practice.

Get a team-mate to act as a partner and, quite simply, try lofting the ball over a distance of 11–16yd (10–15m) to him. As you get better, move further apart. Remember to concentrate on the

MIDFIELD · PLAY

Midfield defence practice.
Lofted passes between the Y's, with the X's closing down the kicker.

Contact for the lofted pass must be with the lower half of the ball.

SOCCER

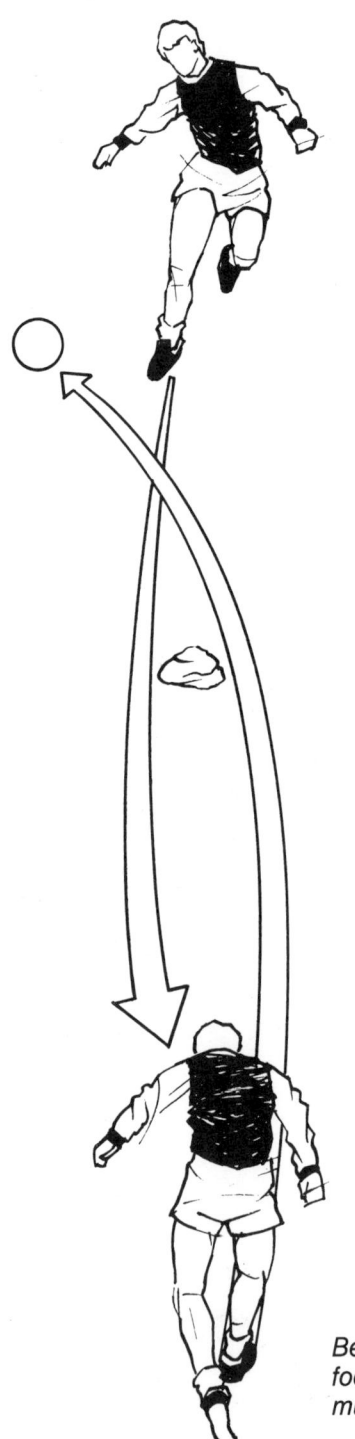

accuracy of the pass. Ideally the ball should land within 2ft (60cm) of your partner.

Now that you have got used to passing accurately you will want to develop your skill further by introducing some 'opposition' to create a game situation.

What we are looking for in the practice is for the Ys to pass the ball over Xs (the defenders). Y1 plays the ball to Y2. When Y2 has had his first touch, defender X2 should move towards him putting pressure on him. X1 does the same at the other end when Y1 controls the ball.

The introduction of a defender will force you to make the pass quicker, but you should still pay particular attention to the accuracy and quality of the pass. The better it is, the easier it is for your partner to control and deliver the ball back to you.

During this practice you will find the defender will present another problem. As he moves towards you (closes you down), he will also block the path of your delivery of the ball. So we now need to look at bending or swerving the ball around him.

Bending and swerving the ball

This type of pass can be achieved in one of two ways; with the inside or the outside of the foot. The choice you make will depend on the line of approach of the defender and the position of the teammate you intend passing to.

In the first instance we will look at bending the ball with the inside of the foot, making sure it actually travels in an arc. If the kick is being made with the right foot the approach should be slightly to the left of the ball. This will allow the foot to move across the ball from the inside to out.

Bending the ball with the inside of the foot. To bend the ball, the striking foot must be moving across the ball.

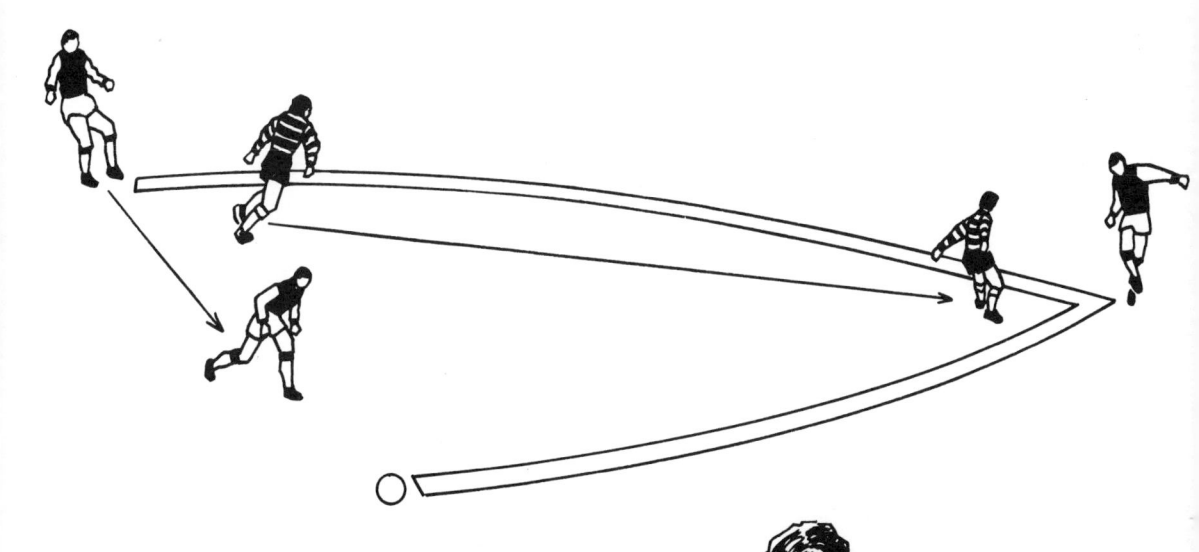

MIDFIELD · PLAY

Bending the ball with the outside of the foot.

Position after the swerving kick.

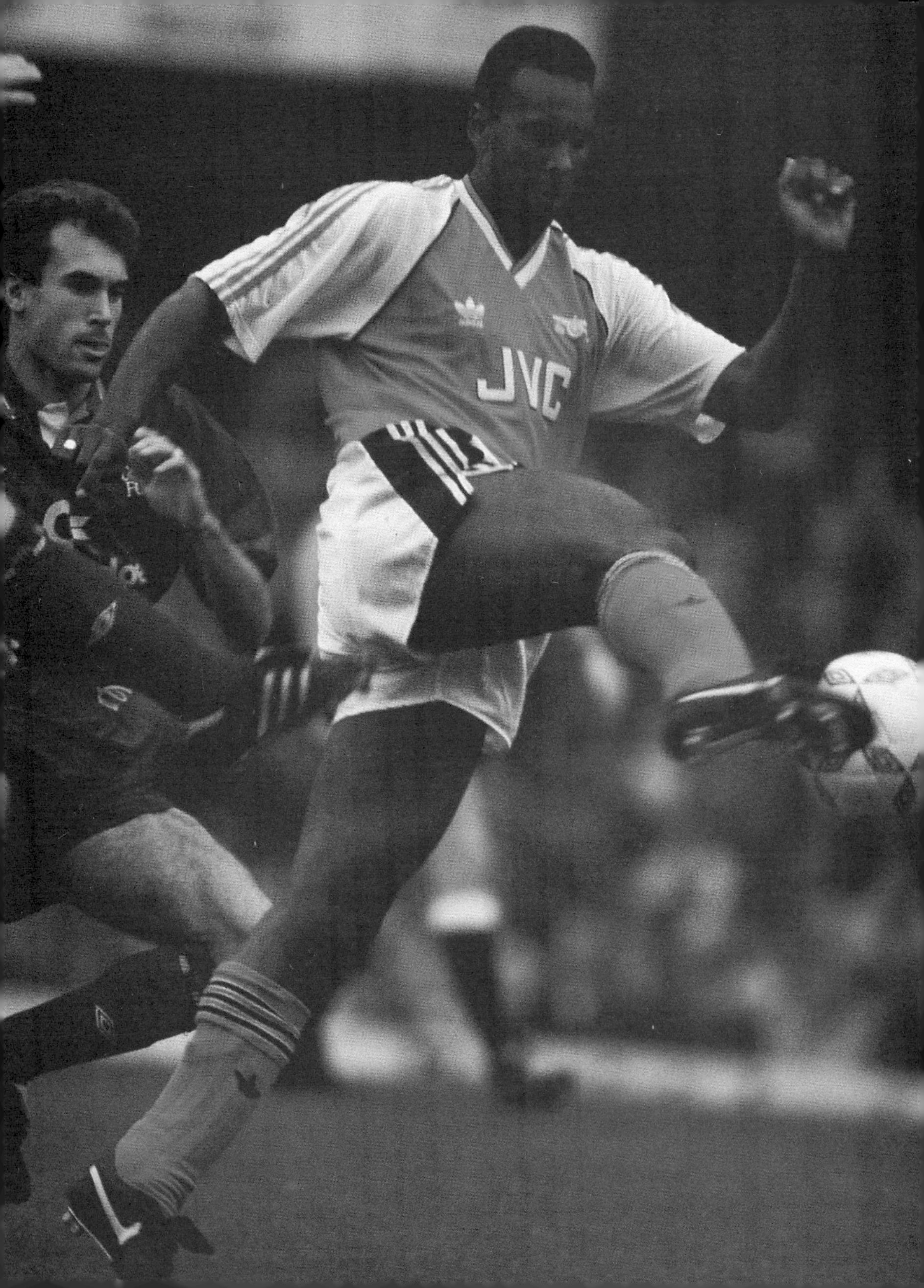
JVC

MIDFIELD · PLAY

Your non-kicking foot should be in a comfortable position to the side of the ball, and your head should be held steady with your eyes looking at the ball. Once more your upper body should be leaning slightly back.

However, as the objective is to bend the ball, contact is made with the front of the foot, in the region of the joint of the big toe, which should strike the ball just right of centre. This is not a full contact, more a slicing action which will create spin and swerve the ball from right to left.

Initially concentrate on bending the pass then, as you improve, increase the distance between you and your partner. As the distances increase you will now have to give the ball a higher trajectory. Contact should still be to the right of the ball but now through the bottom half, and to give it that extra lift you lean back a bit more. Try not to go for too much height on a ball travelling with pace; somewhere between shoulder-height and just above head-height is ideal.

The principles of practice for the bending pass are the same as for the swerve except it is now made with the outside of the foot. Approach to the ball can be virtually straight and your kicking action is across the ball from the inside to the outside. Contact should be made with the outside of the ball through the mid-line. The part of the foot which makes contact should be in the area of the joint of the little toe. At first concentrate on making the ball swerve. As you become more proficient, increase the distance between you and your partner. If you want to lift the ball, strike it lower down and lean back slightly more than normal.

To continue your development, bring defenders into your practice sessions. As

Arsenal's David Rocastle displays the importance of the quality of the first touch when controlling the ball in tight situations.

they close you down, try to bend the ball around them, either with the outside or inside of the foot. Remember you have to try to clear the defender, so you need height and pace on the ball – but don't sacrifice quality and accuracy for it.

The straight pass

By altering your contact with the ball, you can play the ball over players or close to the ground. So, we will finally look at the ball which is driven low and straight.

This pass is harder to make than some players realize. There is a tendency to kick through the bottom half of the ball, as with the lofted pass, when ideally you don't want the ball to rise more than 1ft (30cm) off the ground. Concentrate on pointing your toe straight down to the floor and striking through the vertical centre of the ball with your upper body leaning slightly forward. It is not the easiest of techniques and when practising with a partner you should start by standing reasonably close together and gradually moving further apart as you improve your technique.

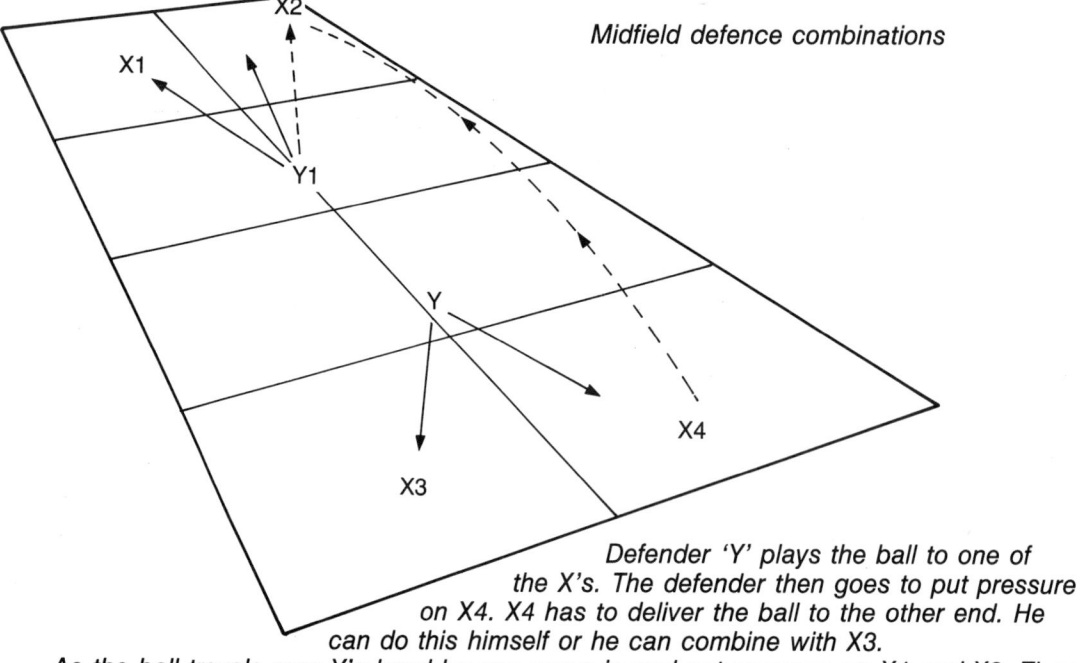

SOCCER

Midfield defence combinations

Defender 'Y' plays the ball to one of the X's. The defender then goes to put pressure on X4. X4 has to deliver the ball to the other end. He can do this himself or he can combine with X3. As the ball travels over Y's head he can move in and put pressure on X1 and X2. They have to control the ball, the object being to deliver the ball to the other end at the earliest opportunity. Lofted, swerved and driven passes should be used whenever possible.

Now you are aware of the different ways of playing the ball over long distances it is up to you to select the correct pass according to the situation you are in. A lot will depend on your first touch and to where it takes you in relation to the defender closing you down and, of course, on how much time you have.

As a final aid to your advancement as a midfield player try the following practice:

This practice gives you the opportunity to play the ball yourself or, if that's not possible, to pass to a team-mate who can then deliver it to the other end of the practice area. The ball can be played through the air, along the ground or with swerve. Only you can make that decision but accuracy and quality must be uppermost in your mind. This practice is ideal for covering all aspects of the passing game.

It is crucial that you practise all the techniques with both feet. Don't forget that long passing is not only about power, but about correct timing and technique.

There are no easy jobs in football. Playing in midfield must be one of the hardest, if not the hardest positions. We have looked at one aspect of the midfielder's game. You need to develop this side of your game. But don't forget you have to concentrate on your attacking and defensive duties as well.

All midfield players will have their strengths and weaknesses. But it is important that you develop an awareness and appreciation of all aspects of the game and become a competent all-round player. If, for example, the opposing side realize that you are far less confident with your left foot, they will exploit this to the full: practise will minimize such weaknesses.

FOUR

ATTACKING PLAY

The role of forward or striker is seen as one of the most glamorous in football today. The ability to score goals has become a priceless commodity, and professional clubs the world over are prepared to pay unbelievable sums of money for players who can score goals.

Goals, however, are the reward for a lot of hard work and effort off the ball. The role of the forward changes constantly. When the opposition wins the ball you have to chase, close down and put them under pressure. When your own team gains possession you have to offer yourself as a target man, holding the ball until support arrives. It requires a lot of running off the ball, both to create openings for others and to get yourself into a scoring position.

To sum up, a striker needs speed and stamina, and strength is required to withstand tackles. The striker also has to be brave and be prepared to go where it hurts to score. Finally the striker needs a good mental attitude to enable him to work alone up front, often for long periods of the game.

When you go to your next game, watch what the front players are doing when play is in other areas of the pitch. Rest assured they will not be standing on the penalty spot waiting for the ball. They will be busy trying to create a scoring opportunity. The vast majority of a striker's work is done outside the penalty area.

BACK · TO · GOAL · TECHNIQUE

Before looking at the art of goal scoring we will first look at the position forward players often find themselves in; with their backs to their opponent's goal.

When receiving the ball you will often find yourself isolated so you will have to hold on to the ball until support from team-mates arrives. This is not always easy. Sometimes the balls are not easy to control, and invariably, you will have a defender in close attendance. You will have a few seconds to control and shield the ball before passing or even turning and possibly beating the defender.

Balls played up to front men vary. It is important, then, that you get in line with the ball and go towards it preventing the defender getting in front of you.

Again it is important to stress the quality of your first touch; playing the ball away from the defender, but keeping as much

SOCCER

of your body between you and him as possible. Once you have the ball under control the defender will try even harder to win possession.

It is at this moment that you need strength and composure. You also have to keep the ball as far away from the defender as possible. Usually you will have controlled the ball with an open body position so you need to quickly change to a side on position. The ball needs to be moved with the outside of the foot furthest away from the defender. For you this is a position of strength with your body weight on your leg nearest the defender and the width of your body between him and the ball.

In this position it's virtually impossible for the defender to get the ball without fouling you. So be patient and use the time to decide your next move.

It is usual when you receive the ball that the space you have to move in will be minimal, so this needs to be reflected in the practice.

We can start quite simply with two players in a 10m (10yd) square, or use the centre circle of the pitch. X1 plays the ball into X2 positioned in the square. He has to control and shield the ball from defender Y2. This can be for a set period of time, say 20/30 seconds, or for the time

To shield the ball, receive it in an open body position, and quickly move to the side-on position, using the foot furthest away from the defender.

ATTACKING · PLAY

Feinting to go one way, player moves onto right shoulder.

it takes X1 to run around the square. After that the ball can be played out to him. The roles can be reversed amongst the three players.

As you progress, so the area should change. The centre circle can be used for receiving the ball and the players can be restricted to that area.

The distance and type of service from the third player should always vary, playing through the air and along the floor.

You may be able to take the ball with the outside of the foot in the side-on position, depending on the quality of the pass.

You can lay the ball off to a supporting player or you can in one movement turn,

SOCCER

ATTACKING · PLAY

and go past the player marking you. This exercise is particularly beneficial for those occasions when you receive the ball in and around the penalty area.

Beating the defender

The methods of beating a defender when you have your back to the goal are basically a mirror image of those used when you are facing him. You can feint or dummy to go one way but go the opposite way. Or you can perform a trick. In both cases you are trying to move or unbalance the defender.

If we first look at the feint we can assume you have the ball under control and are in a good position shielding the ball. With the defender close behind you, we want him to believe you are going to turn outside. Bend your knees slightly and move all of your body to your outside. Speed is now so important. With the same foot, turn the ball to attack the space inside the defender. Depending on the closeness of the defender you may be able to move the ball with your other foot.

If you are shielding the ball with the right, feint to go outside then quickly get your left foot behind the ball and with the outside of the foot turn the ball inside the defender.

Ideally it is best to perform the turn without actually stopping the ball. As the ball is coming to you, step towards it putting all your weight on the leading foot. Allow the ball to travel past the leading foot, turn the ball inside the defender with your other foot. Again bend the knees to adopt a low body position which will provide you with the explosive thrust to burst past the defender.

The trick is again about making the defender believe you are going to do one

Having committed the defender, pace which allows you to get away is essential, as Argentina's Diego Maradona shows.

thing when, of course, you intend doing the opposite.

The particular trick we will look at is known as the 'Cruyff turn' which was perfected by the former Dutch international Johan Cruyff.

With your back to the goal and the defender in close attendance, using your right foot move as though you are going to turn to your left or play a ball to your left. This will usually move the defender onto your left shoulder. With your right foot, pull the ball inside your standing leg, pushing the ball behind you and past the defender. Again you must turn or spin quickly and explode past the defender.

Practise these moves on your own first. Start slowly and try the moves with both feet. As your confidence grows try the following practice with team mates.

This is similar to the previous practice, but we are now looking for Y2 to turn and get past defender X2 and have a shot at goal. The balls played into the central players should be varied; along the floor, bouncing, and in the air.

We have looked at just a couple of moves here, but watch the top players and see how they deal with the situation. Manchester United's Mark Hughes is an excellent example of a striker shielding the ball and then turning or laying it off.

No matter what level of football you watch or play in, the forward players will get the ball with their backs to the goal more than in any other position. So it is important that you work on this aspect of your game.

SOCCER

Attacking play.
The 'Cruyff' turn. Turn your right foot inward with the toe down and push the ball behind and away from you.

ATTACKING · PLAY

Getting past defence.
Area: 10 yd (9 m) × 30 yd (27 m)
Y1 plays ball to Y2. Y2 has to turn past X1 and try to score past X2.

For this trick, move the defender to one side, allow the ball to run across the body. Then move the ball with the outside of the left foot, spin quickly and explode past the defender on the inside.

SOCCER

Turning using the inside of the foot.

SHOOTING · TECHNIQUES

Having successfully turned and got past the defender you could be in a position to have a strike on goal. It's important you take the opportunity to shoot. The reason comes down to simple mathematics: the more often you shoot the more often you will score.

So much will be going through your mind at this moment. Foremost should be to hit the target. Sadly, too many players go for power before accuracy and don't even force the goalkeeper to make a save. When you get your shot in, you want to make life as difficult as possible for the 'keeper. You can do this by keeping the shot low. Shots in and around chest height are easy for goalkeepers to handle, while ground shots provide many problems. As well as requiring time to 'get down' to the shot, the ball can also bobble and skid on its way through.

You can practise this aspect of your game either on your own or as in the following practice.

In the practice the Xs take turns to shoot at the goal remembering to concentrate on accuracy and keeping the shot low. When receiving the ball, the Xs should play the ball slightly out to their feet. At this moment they should look up and assess the goalkeeper's position. When you strike the ball your head should be steady and looking at the ball. The contact with the ball should be with the instep and through the mid-line of the ball. Concentrate initially on hitting the target and keeping the ball low. As you develop, begin to pick your most favoured spot

ATTACKING · PLAY

to beat the goalkeeper.

In this practice you will find that your shooting position is not always in the centre of the goal. When you are in a position wide of centre you should aim to shoot across the goalkeeper. Using the same practice arrangements, with your first touch take the ball to one side of the goal. If the goalkeeper has correctly assessed his angles, the hardest place to score will be at the near post, therefore your aim should be for the far post. This is a difficult shot for the 'keeper to save. If he does get a hand to the ball it often leads to a secondary scoring chance. By this we mean the 'keeper will only be able to palm the ball back into play, creating the possibility of a simple tap in goal for a fellow striker. Driving the ball across goal creates more options than trying for the near post; deflections, own goals and corners are just a few of the possible benefits.

Try the following practice.

The practice is started with X1 playing the ball to X2 in a wide position. X2 can strike the ball first time or with his second touch, but it must be across the goal to the far post area. After playing the ball X1 must look to attack the area in and around the far post. He must be careful not to go past X2 before he shoots; the possibility in a game is that he could be offside. His movements have to be quick and he must be prepared to punish deflections off the 'keeper or the post.

There are many ways of scoring goals but these basic principles will nearly always apply when you are shooting for goal. As a large proportion of goals are scored from within the 18 yard box, the following practice will help you to appreciate the opportunities which may arise. Success depends very much on your reactions and improvisations.

Play is confined to the 18 yard box where the pairs play against each other; the goalkeeper is neutral. If the ball goes

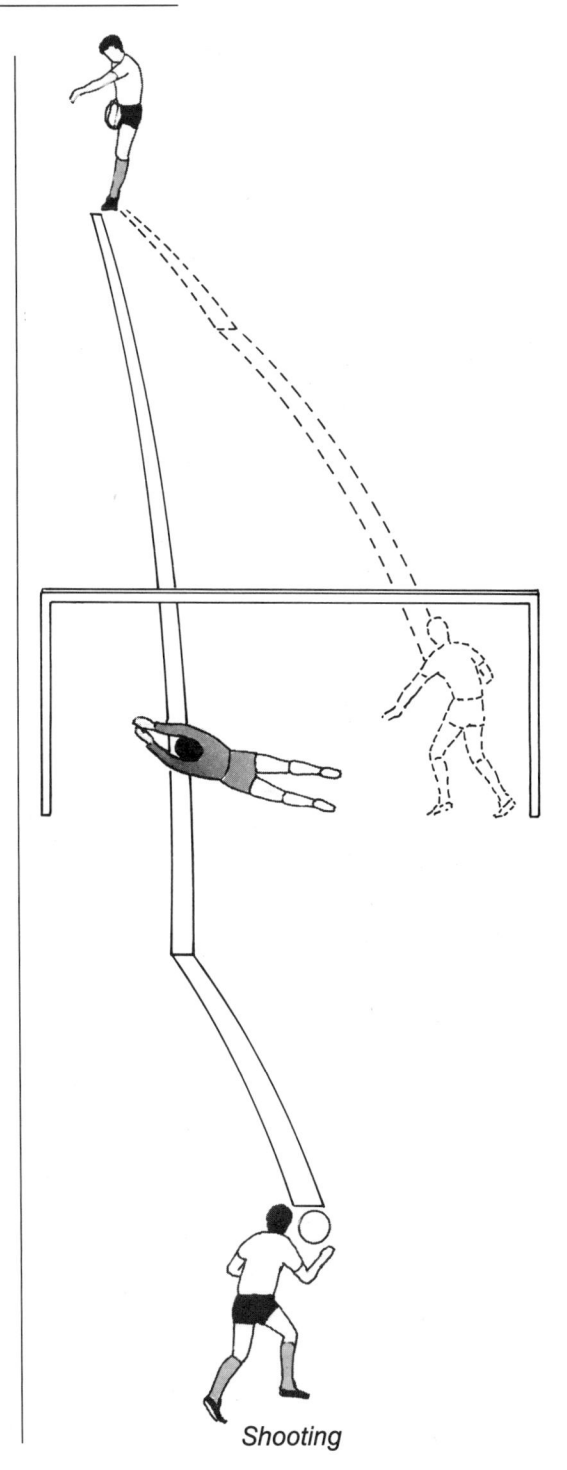

Shooting

SOCCER

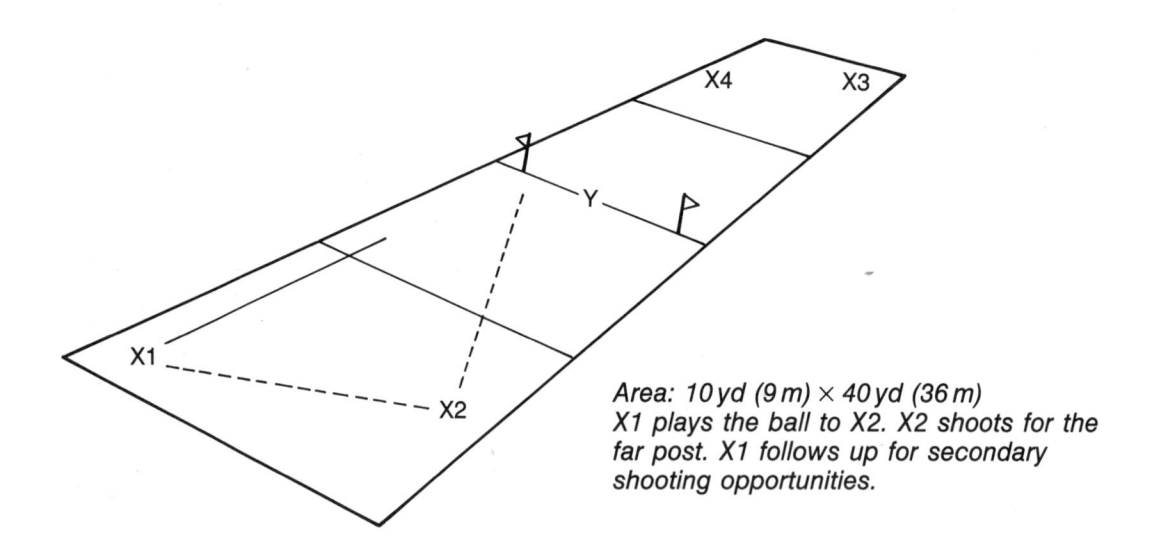

Area: 10 yd (9 m) × 40 yd (36 m)
X1 plays the ball to X2. X2 shoots for the far post. X1 follows up for secondary shooting opportunities.

out of the area the nearest player to the ball takes a throw-in. The goalkeeper should also throw the ball in and he should vary the service.

The players will quickly find that time and space is limited and on most occasions they will not have time to control the ball. They need to get into line with the ball and be prepared to take their shooting opportunities as early as possible. This could require you to volley the ball as it travels through the air and to make the necessary body-position adjustments in respect to the height of the ball.

The half-volley

Striking the ball on the half-volley is another way of taking opportunities early. This occurs when the ball has just touched the ground and then nicely sits up and invites a shot.

Play is restricted to the 18 yd box, and pairs combine to score. Rebounds/secondary scoring chances go to the first player to react. The goalkeeper is neutral and should deliver the ball to empty spaces.

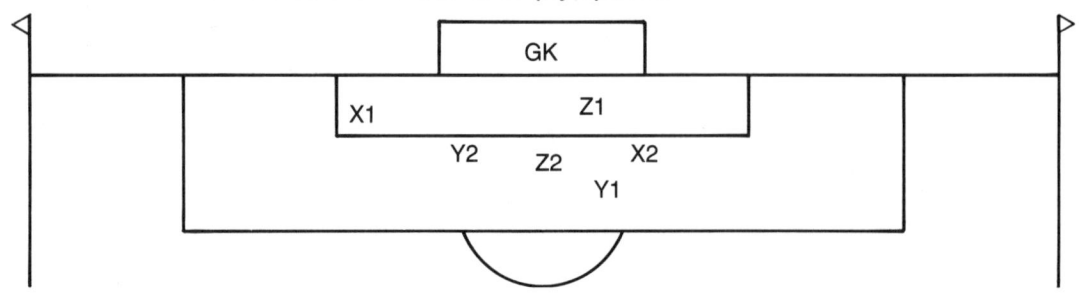

ATTACKING · PLAY

England's Chris Waddle's repertoire of tricks and feints makes him a constant problem for defenders.

SOCCER

In a crowded goalmouth, forwards who are marked tight generally don't get time to swing their leg in situations like this so you should be happy to get a toe or foot to the ball and just poke it in the right direction.

Finally we have improvization, which usually produces the spectacular goals. Real Madrid's Hugo Sanchez regularly performs the overhead bicycle kick, and the equally impressive side volley with which Mark Hughes scored for Wales against Spain in 1985 are two examples of improvization producing spectacular goals.

But there are other forms of improvization. It could be a shot bent around defenders or chipped over the goalkeeper. Or it could be a 'cheeky' back-heel.

It doesn't matter how you score; all goals are good goals. But the same basic principles will always apply: (a) be accurate – hit the target (b) keep the ball low, and (c) almost always shoot for the far post.

Heading

It is not always possible to get your leg or foot to the ball – perhaps because of the height or the angle at which the ball comes to you – but you can't let the opportunity pass just because you are not in a comfortable position to strike with your foot. So, you must now attack the ball with your head.

A large number of goals are scored with the head and the biggest strength of England internationals Mick Hartford and Mark Hateley lies in this area.

Before we look at the actual technique required when heading for goal it's worth mentioning the player's mental attitude. You have got to be brave, be prepared to be 'clattered' by goalkeepers or defenders. You also have to be quick-thinking; if you stop to think about it then

Y throws or crosses the ball for X to head at the far post.

the chance could be lost. So with a good mental approach, it's then a combination of concentration and timing of your run that you need to practise.

It is not impossible, but it is very difficult, to head a ball if you are standing waiting and have to jump straight-up. Ideally you want to be running onto the ball. The speed of the run will provide you with the

ATTACKING · PLAY

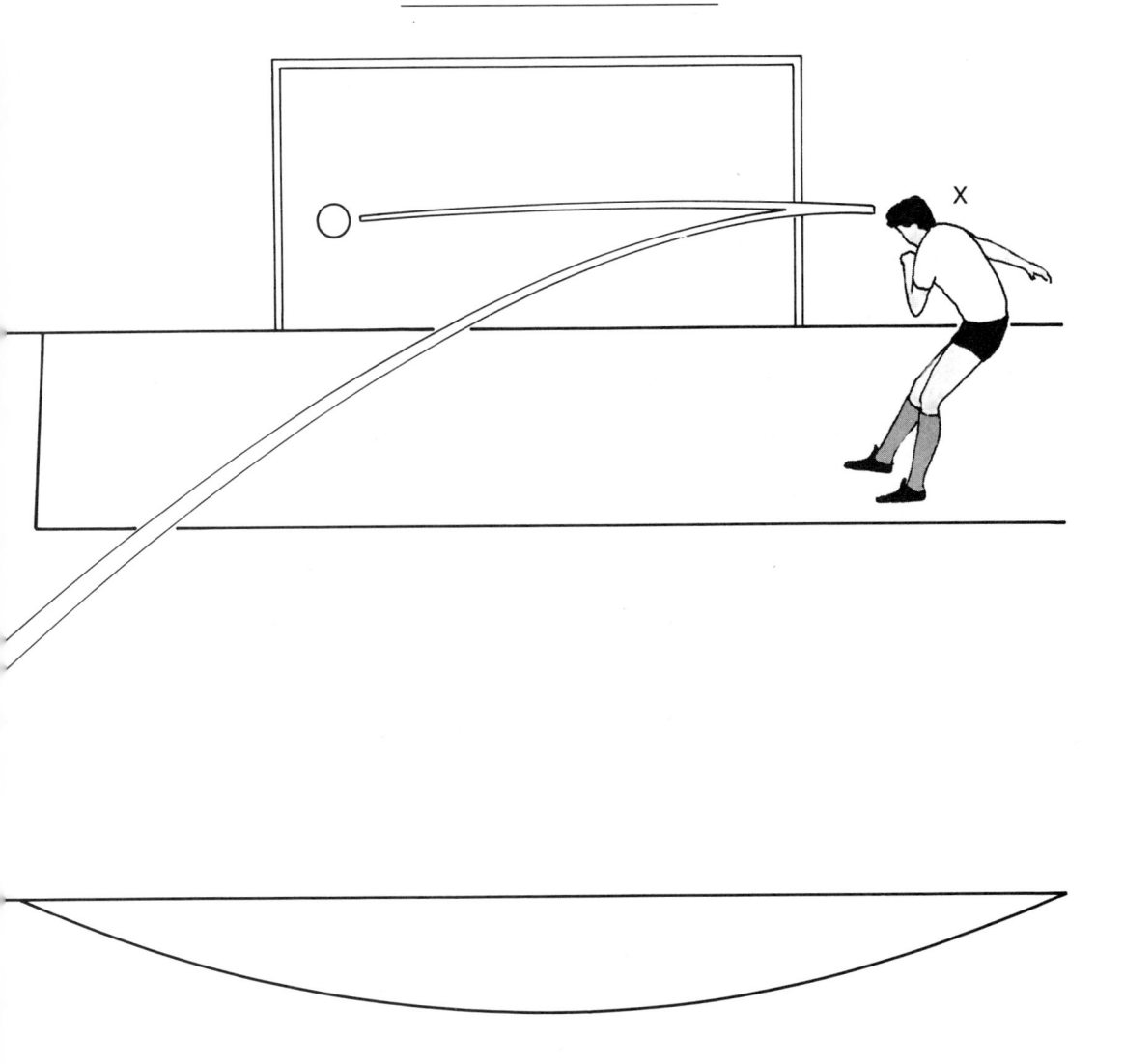

momentum to gain height when leaping upwards. It will also add to the power of the header.

You need to concentrate on the flight of the ball and aim to make contact with the ball at the highest point of your leap. Contact should be made with the forehead and added power can be gained by arching your back and neck muscles. Again you can practise with a team mate. Get him to toss the ball in the air. Concentrate on the ball, time your run, and make good contact with your head.

It was once the case that players were always told to head the ball down, but circumstances and position dictate where the ball is to be headed. What should be uppermost in your mind is that you aim to

SOCCER

Head for goal technique.

ATTACKING · PLAY

hit the target. Your contact should always be through the middle of the ball, rather than heading through the lower half which will often cause the ball to go sailing over the top of the cross bar.

The majority of headed goals come from crosses, so we will now alter our practice so we can appreciate the problems crosses will present to you.

Begin with Y throwing the ball across the goal. One of the first things you will appreciate is the actual area in which you will usually make contact with the ball. The crosses (throws for the time being) will be away from the 'keeper so it's reasonable to expect you will be making contact around the far post area. When heading from this position it's often beneficial to head back across the goal towards the opposite post as this will force the goalkeeper to change direction.

As the practice progresses, Y should begin crossing the ball with his feet. This will help create match-like conditions and help you to improve your timing and runs. It will also make you aware of the need for improvization. Not all crosses will land just where you would like them to.

One of the more spectacular headed goals is the improvized diving header which calls for a great deal of bravery in an area where boots are often flying in all directions!

The diving header is often an instinctive reaction to a cross which has come in low or dropped suddenly. Keep your eye on the ball, attack it, make a good contact and, most importantly, hit the target.

To practise the diving header go back to the last two practice sessions but this time get the player Y to supply the ball low. At first you will probably worry about your landing, but this becomes an enjoyable practice once that fear is overcome.

Diving header.

Up to now we have looked at headed goals in the area around the far post. But in today's game headers at the near post can also bring the highest rewards.

Watching the flight of the ball and timing your run are two of the key factors. The contact with the ball, however, is not as firm as it was with the far post header. If the run is timed correctly then your position at the point of contact will be level, or just in front of the near post within the six-yard box. As you will be moving towards the ball, the ball needs only to brush against your forehead, which will usually deflect it in the direction of the far post.

Holland's Ruud Gullit emphasizes the importance of the near post corner in today's game, as he creates danger with a ball flicked across the face of the goal.

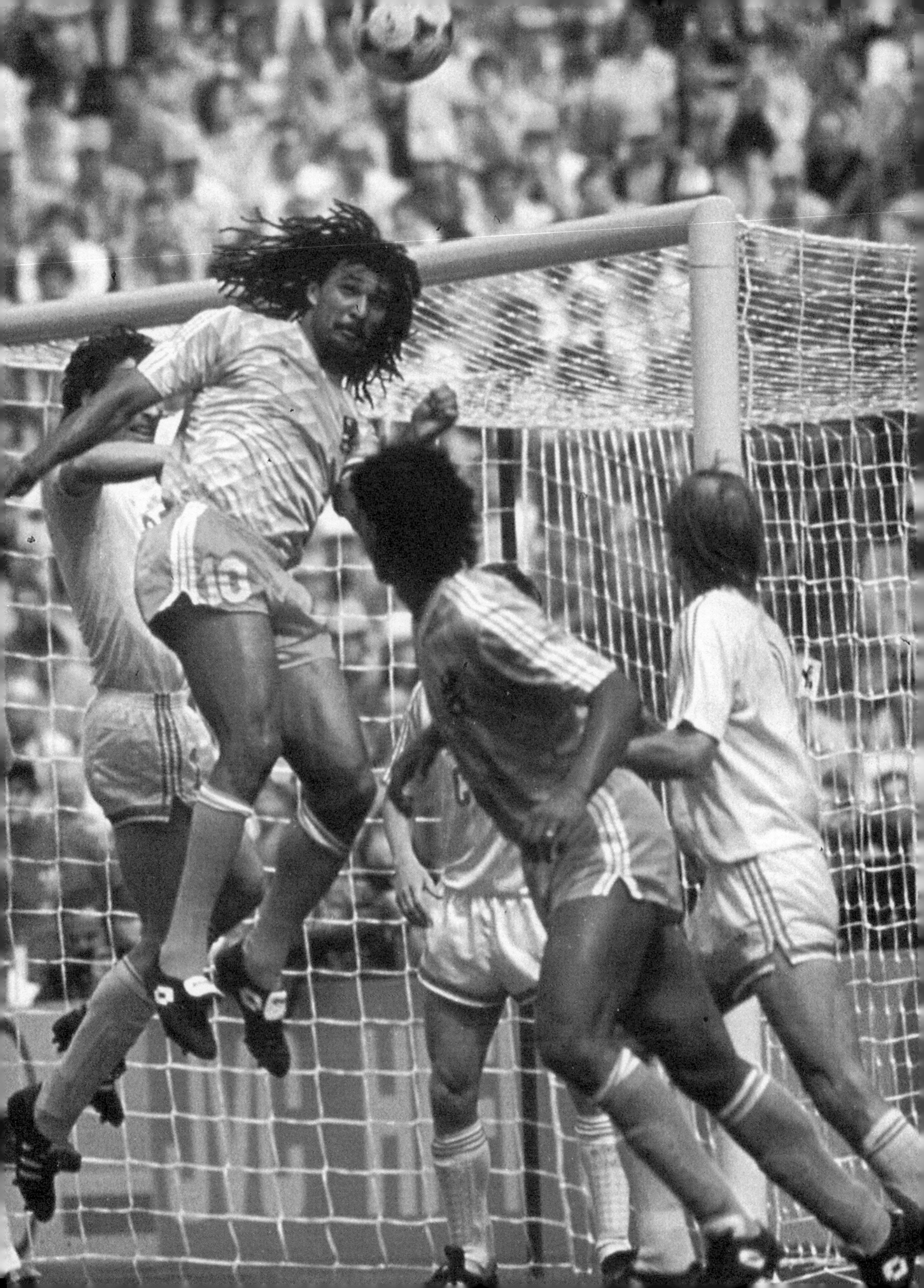

SOCCER

The near post header.

This is a very difficult ball to defend. Even if the actual header does not hit the target, it will provide scoring opportunities for other in rushing forwards.

As we said at the beginning, scoring goals is one of the most exciting aspects of the game. To some players it appears to come naturally and to a certain degree that is true, because their mental attitude is right. They are single-minded. All they want to do is score goals, but it requires lots of work off the ball to create the scoring opportunities. Also, hours are spent on the practice ground working on routines and getting the timing right. So, next time you see the likes of Gary Lineker scoring 'opportunist' goals, remember how much work has gone into that moment.

Also, next time you go to a game, watch the forwards when they haven't got the ball and notice how they are manoeuvring themselves into goalscoring positions. To be a successful goalscorer it takes strength, pace, skill and ability, and it takes heart and character, especially when things are not going well. That's why clubs pay millions of pounds for players who have that precious ability to score goals.

FIVE

GOALKEEPING

The art of goalkeeping has come a long way in the last twenty years. Gone are the days when it was felt you 'had to be mad' to play in goal. In today's modern game the goalkeeper's role is much respected and regarded as one of the most specialised positions of a team. It is a position that requires a particular blend of temperament: quick reflexes, an ability to predict the pattern of play, and courage when going for the ball.

Stopping goals is still the number one priority of a 'keeper. But he is also expected to organise the defence and often act as an extra defender, and quickly set up attacks with his distribution.

With this in mind top goalkeepers like Peter Shilton, Neville Southall, Bruce Grobbelaar and Jim Leighton spend many hours practising and perfecting all aspects of their game. When he was starting his career at Leicester City, Peter Shilton would stay for hours practising with a forward long after the rest of the players had finished their training for the day. That is what makes a good goalkeeper and a good professional. Those hours of extra practice are still keeping 'Shilts' at the top even after attaining the age of forty.

While the transfer market reflects the importance of the goal-scorers, the value of the man who can stop goals has increased substantially in recent years.

In this chapter we will look at the vital areas of goalkeeping. But the key to the practices is that they are practised at all levels from schoolboy to international level.

HANDLING

Probably the number one requirement of a goalkeeper is that he has a good pair of hands. He needs to be confident and competent in his handling of the ball. One of the simplest and most beneficial ways of improving handling techniques is to get a team-mate to throw or kick the ball at varying heights at the goalkeeper.

Before we actually discuss handling there is a stance (or poise) that goalkeepers should adopt when they are preparing to accept a shot.

Your feet should be about shoulder width apart with your body weight slightly forward on the soles of the feet. Your arms should be slightly to the side of the body, with hands about waist high with the palms facing the kicker. Your head should be steady and leaning slightly forward. This stance is probably best illustrated when a goalkeeper is facing a penalty kick.

Try to adopt this position each time you are waiting to receive a throw or kick from your team-mate in the practice session. The service should be varied with the ball being played to: (i) the area around your feet, (ii) at waist height, and (iii) in and around head and shoulder height. Each of these areas will require you to use different techniques when handling the ball.

Ground shots can be dealt with in one of two ways. Probably the most common, and safest method, is the kneeling technique.

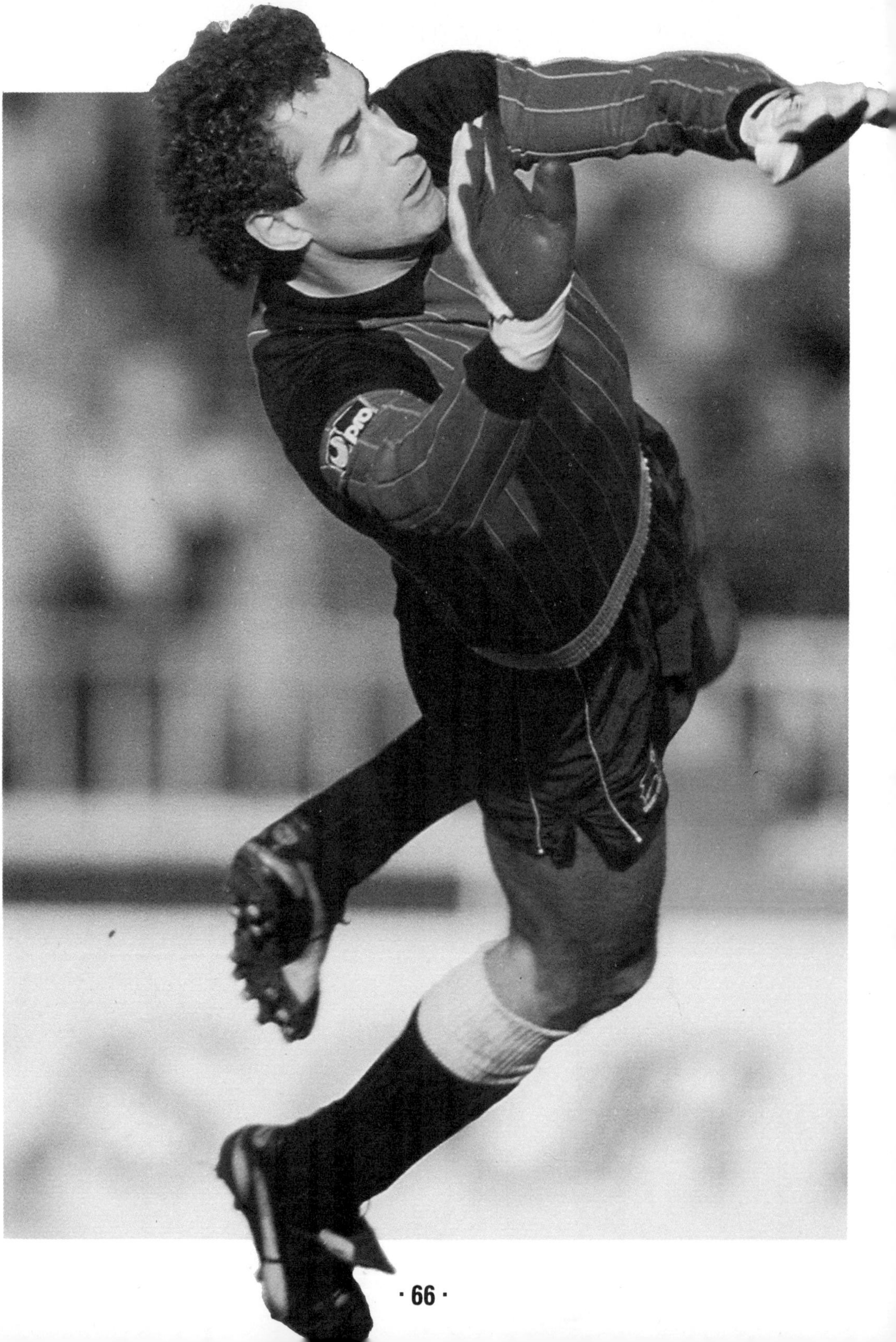

GOALKEEPING

The kneeling technique.

England's Peter Shilton at full stretch. A firm wrist allows him to deflect the ball wide.

SOCCER

Kneeling technique

Using this technique you are able to get more of your body behind the ball. Your left leg needs to be turned sideways to your upper body. Your right knee should be positioned directly behind your left heel forming a sort of 'K' with your body. Your hands should collect the ball in front of you and the ball be quickly transferred to the body. Collecting the ball in front has two advantages: (i) should it slip through your hands you have the added safety of your right thigh as further protection, and (ii) you will be leaning forward thus allowing you to fall on to the ball should it break loose.

You can practise the kneeling technique without a ball. As you practise it will come more naturally and you will feel comfortable and happy using it. Again practise with both the left and right hand side of the body.

Stooping technique

The other technique requires a more upright position and requires you to stoop to collect the ball. Your legs should be kept close together, creating a solid barrier behind your hands. You should collect the ball in front of you and quickly scoop it into your body.

There is little room for error with this technique, but as a goalkeeper you need to practise both ways and decide which is the most comfortable and safest for you.

Waist height shots

With shots around waist height the important thing is to get your body behind the ball. Your arms should be out in front of you to meet the ball and pull it into

"Stooping" technique

GOALKEEPING

your stomach. Once the ball has passed over your hands they should wrap around the ball and securely hold it.

Head height shots

Shots above or around head height require the hands to spread to the side and behind the ball. You should try to form a 'W' shape with the thumbs almost together at the rear of the ball. Again always try to take the ball in front of you, enabling you to see and react quickly should you drop it. You shouldn't need telling what problems you will have if you drop the ball behind you!

It will help if your fingers are relaxed. If they are rigid there is more danger of your dropping the ball on impact. Once you have gathered the ball it should be lowered quickly and securely into the lower part of the body.

The more you practise, the better your handling will become and so your confidence will grow, but remember to get behind the ball as quickly as possible and make sure you keep your eyes on it right up to the time it is securely in your hands.

DIVING

Not all shots are all going to be so easy to deal with and there are times when you are going to have to dive for the ball. The danger, however, is that you begin diving for everything – which is not necessary. If you watch the likes of Southall and Shilton they make difficult saves look easy by quickly moving their feet in order to avoid

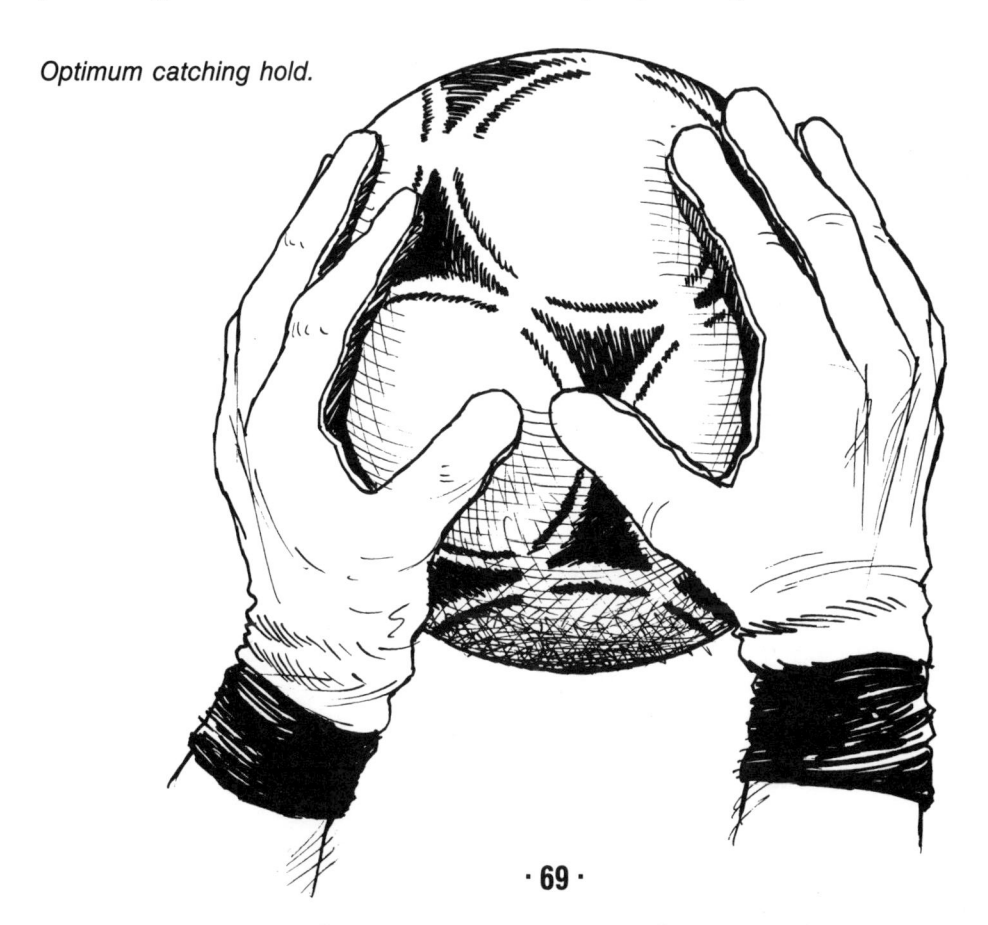

Optimum catching hold.

SOCCER

Move quickly across the line as the ball travels towards the goal.

Get the feet out of the way, the upper body falling out-stretched.

The nearest hand to the ground stops the ball, the other hand on the top. The ball is then pulled into the body.

GOALKEEPING

To reach the ball over waist height, push off with the leg nearest the ball.

having to dive full stretch for shots. This reduces the obvious dangers of dropping the ball and deflecting balls for corners or to the feet of in-rushing forwards.

To practise your diving techniques use the session as before, recruiting the aid of a team-mate. This time, your opponent should play the ball to the corners, beginning with balls played along the ground. Ground shots are probably the most difficult to deal with. You first need to get across your goal-line as quickly as possible while the ball is moving. It then becomes a case of dropping or collapsing to save the ball. Get your feet quickly out from underneath you, with your upper body falling out-stretched onto your side. The hand nearest to the ground should be the one that stops the ball, with your other hand coming over and clamping on top of the ball. Once in this position, you should again move the ball quickly into your body. However, if the player feeding balls to you puts in a weak shot which does not require a dive then don't dive just for the sake of it. Gather the ball in either of the other acceptable manners instead.

Often you are not going to be able to hold the ball and on these occasions you should deflect it wide of your goal. Again you need to cover the ground quickly and contact with the ball should be made with the hand nearest the ground. The contact should be with an open palm and the wrist needs to be firm when directing the ball wide of the goal, which is often at the expense of a corner – but that's better than conceding a goal.

SOCCER

The mistake often made when palming the ball away is that contact is too firm and the ball is directed back into play thus giving the attacking team a secondary goal scoring opportunity. So, always deflect the ball wide.

Shots above waist height give the goalkeeper a better chance of making a diving save. Quick movements of the feet will help you and when you dive it will require a sharp little push-off with the leg nearest to the ball. Where possible you should try and hold the ball, with your hands spread around it. Then, as you fall to the ground, you should try and pull the ball into your body avoiding the danger of it bouncing loose on impact with the ground.

As with the ground shots it's not always possible to hold the ball and once again the need may be to deflect. The aim should be to deflect high and wide of the goal. Depending on how quickly you have moved to the ball this can be done with one or two hands. Try to make the contact in front of you; contact once the ball has passed you increases the chance of deflecting it into your own goal.

The top goalkeepers make things look easy. They don't elaborate. They all stick to the following principles which you should adopt:

(a) Keep things simple.
(b) Keep your eye on the ball.
(c) Get your body behind the shot where possible.
(d) Move your feet quickly to cover the ground.

By correctly positioning himself, a goalkeeper can cut down the distance he has to cover and also make it difficult for the opposing forward to score.

POSITIONING

The goalkeeper needs to adjust his position in relation to the position of the ball. The first priority of the keeper is to position himself in line with the ball. He must then determine which is the most vulnerable part of the goal and get himself into the best position to protect it. Finally, the closer he is to the ball the less the forward can see of the goal. So, having positioned himself in line with the ball he must decide how far he can move down the line. The further the forward is from the goal the further from the goal the goalkeeper can move. However, he should not come too far down the line because then the ball can be chipped or lobbed over his head.

The following practice will provide numerous opportunities to assess your angles.

GK1 throws the ball out to X1 who has to control and shoot with his second touch. As X1 prepares to shoot GK2 should quickly get into the line of the ball. If X's position is wide to the right of the goal then GK2 should position himself where he can protect his near post. Again depending on how far out X1 is, the 'keeper may need to shuffle down the line towards the forward.

The practice continues with GK2 giving the ball to Y1 or Y2 who repeats the sequence against GK1.

Once you have decided you are in the correct position you need to hold your ground, be confident, composed and stay big. In other words, don't make the forward's mind up by diving or going to ground: wait for him to make the decision.

Good concentration and mental awareness help make Everton's Neville Southall one of the world's top goalkeepers.

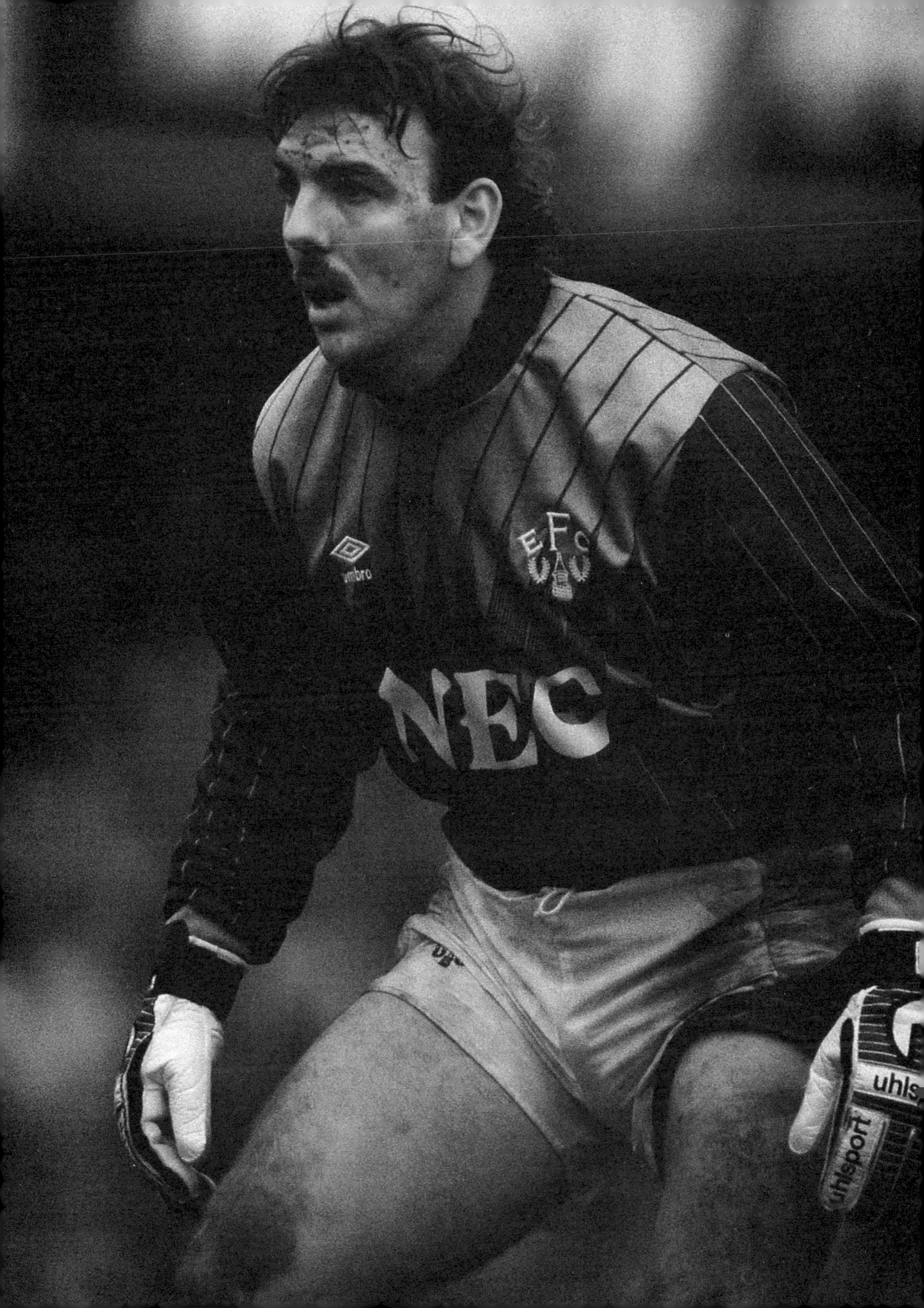
EFC
umbro
NEC
uhlsport

SOCCER

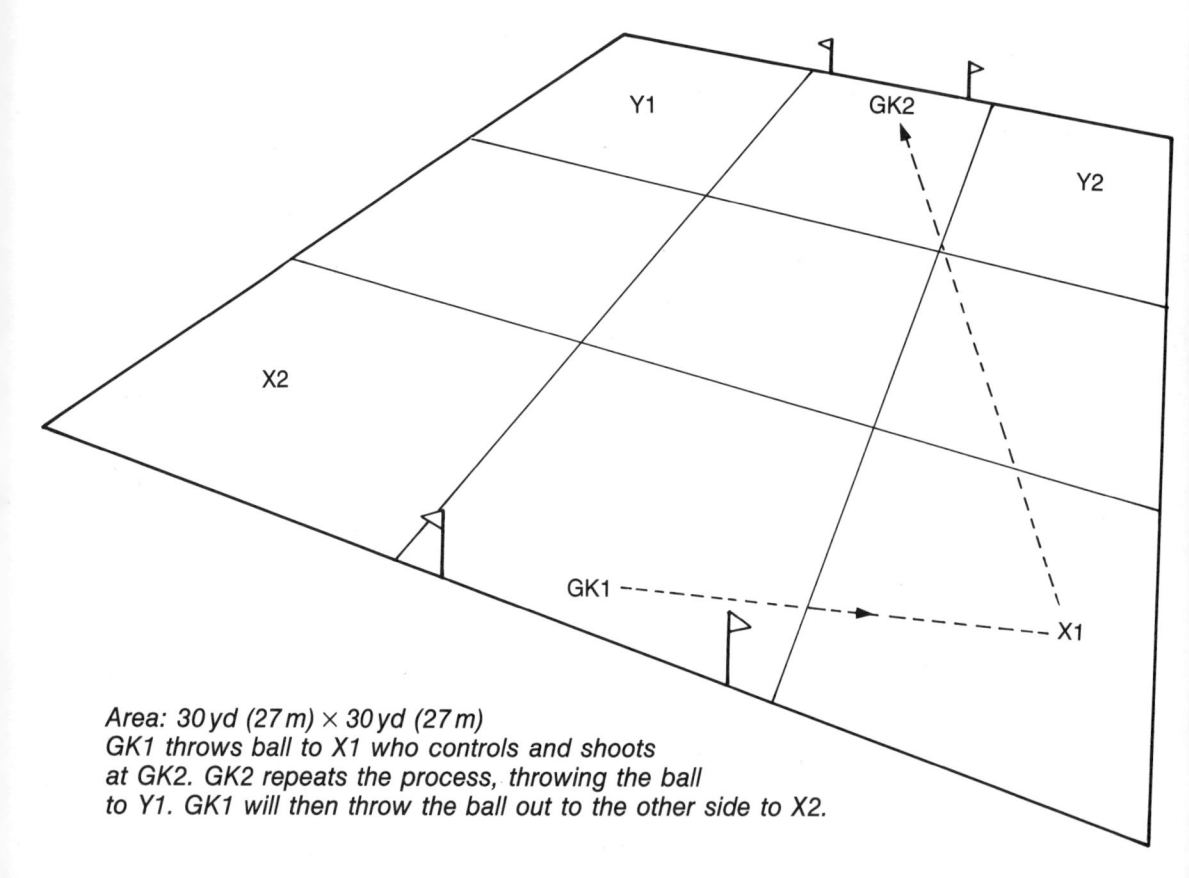

Area: 30 yd (27 m) × 30 yd (27 m)
GK1 throws ball to X1 who controls and shoots at GK2. GK2 repeats the process, throwing the ball to Y1. GK1 will then throw the ball out to the other side to X2.

If we allow the outfield player as many touches as he wants, inevitably he will take the ball closer to the 'keeper. It then becomes a battle of wits between the two players. If you, as the 'keeper, have got your angles right then your priority is to force the forward wide of the goal. A slight adjustment of your body position will invite this. In this position the forward will have to consider his options and for a split second he may glance down at the ball or at the goal. It is at this moment that you need to commit yourself. Spread your body across the ground in front of the player with the ball. Even if you are unable to collect the ball you will probably force him even wider. Also, he may lose control of the ball. In both cases you will have bought time, allowing defenders perhaps, to clear the lines.

Remember to stand up as long as you can, don't commit yourself too early and always force the attacker wide.

CROSSES

While shot-stopping is probably the most important aspect of goalkeeping, handling and the ability to deal comfortably with crosses is a key factor in the development of a 'keeper. Dealing with crosses requires concentration, good judgement technique and, of course, courage when under pressure from the opposition.

GOALKEEPING

When diving at a forward's feet, force him wide, then spread yourself.

SOCCER

Always force the forward wide of the goal.

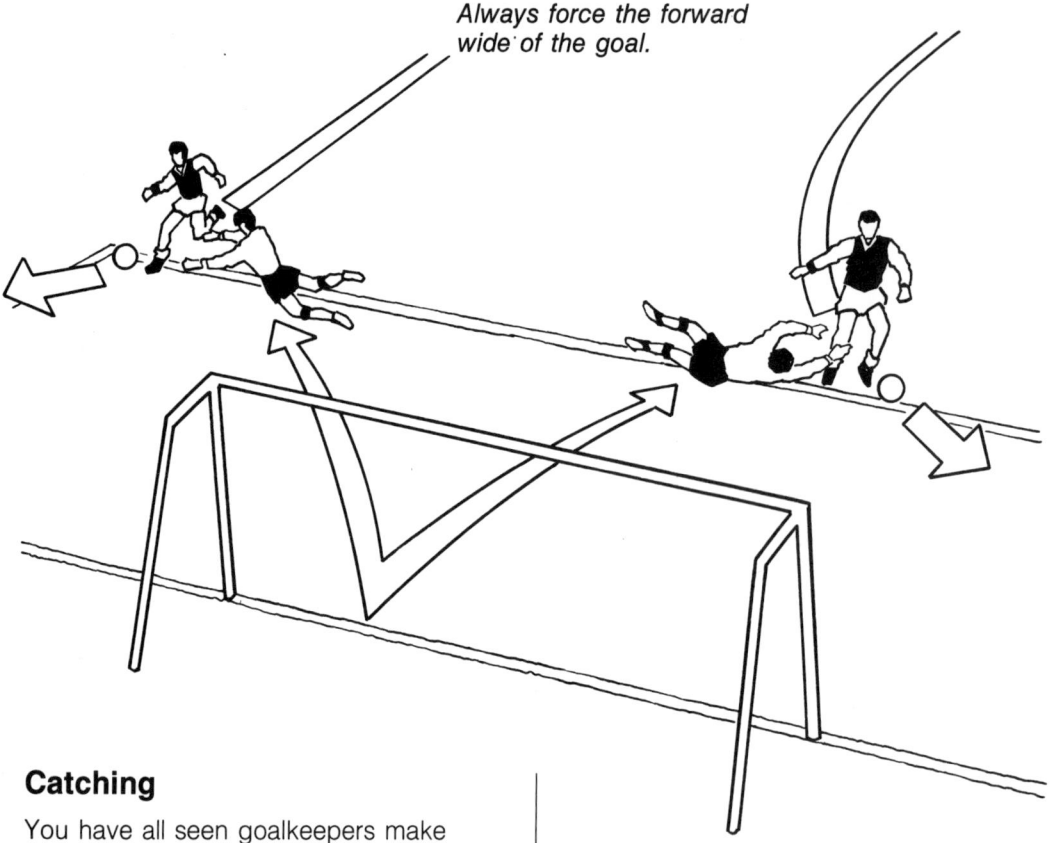

Catching

You have all seen goalkeepers make good clean catches. But what you often don't see is the initial preparation required.

That begins with the goalkeeper's position and his stance. As a simple rule; the nearer the halfway line the ball is, then the further you can be out of your goal.

The goalkeeper should have an open body position, and the line of his shoulders should be parallel with the goal line, allowing him vision through 180°. This gives him the advantage of seeing runs which may be made by an attacking player to the near post. From this position, he can assess the flight of the ball.

You must wait for the ball to be kicked; do not anticipate. Once it has been kicked you need to consider three factors: (a) the line along which the ball is travelling, (b) the pace and trajectory of the ball, and (c) any swerve or dip on it.

You must then make an early decision as to whether you are going to attack the cross. If you are, you should ensure that your route to the ball is not impeded. Aim to catch the ball at the highest possible point. It will help if you leave your move for the ball as late as possible. This will give you more time to assess the flight of the ball. When you do go for the ball you will have to move quickly but this will provide you with greater momentum for your upward leap.

To achieve the greatest possible height your take off should be from one foot: this is a smooth natural technique which gives you good balance. As we said you need to catch the ball at the highest possible

· 76 ·

GOALKEEPING

Assess the flight of the ball, and catch it at the highest possible point.

SOCCER

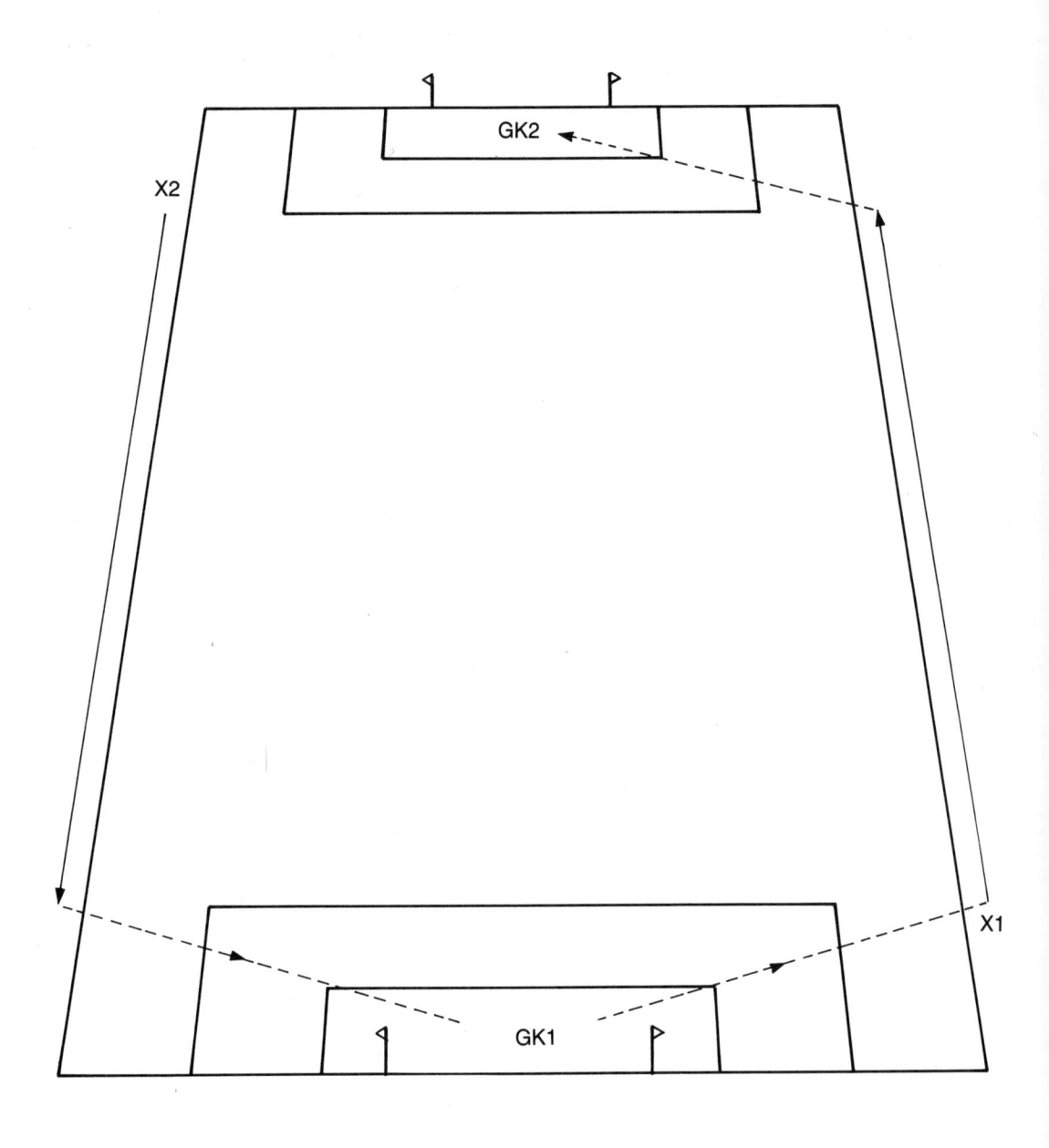

Area: One penalty area and another goal approx 40 yd (36 m) away.
GK1 throws the ball out to X1, who runs the ball down the line and crosses for GK2 to deal with. GK2 then feeds the ball out to X2 to repeat the process.

GOALKEEPING

The two-fisted clearance.

point, this is where you have the biggest advantage over the attacking players because you can use your arms which should be outstretched and the catch should be made in front of the head with the hands once again in the 'W' position. Once the catch is made the ball should be brought into the body as quickly as possible.

Try the following practice. It will provide you with a variety of opportunities to deal with many different crosses.

The practice begins with GK1 throwing the ball out to X1 who moves down the line and crosses the ball for GK2 to catch. Once he has caught the ball he should throw it to X2 who repeats the procedure to GK1. The players crossing the ball should be encouraged and reminded to vary the crosses to near and far posts. The practice can also be reversed, allowing GK the opportunity to deal with crosses from the left.

As with all other aspects of the game, it is important that practice routines offer as much variety as possible.

SOCCER

The one-fisted clearance.

Punching

Ideally, when a goalkeeper comes for a cross he should catch it. However, that is not always possible. In such instances it is usual for the 'keeper to punch or deflect the ball away.

When there is a possibility of a challenge, the goalkeeper may elect to punch. This should be done with two fists, giving you a greater area of contact with the ball; and you should strike through the bottom half of the ball ensuring you get height and distance on the clearance. The two-fisted technique is most beneficial when you have opponents or defenders in front of you. A good example is when dealing with a corner played to the near post.

There are occasions when you will use just one fist. This usually occurs when you are attacking the ball across the line of flight. You are basically helping the ball on

· 80 ·

GOALKEEPING

its way but clearing it away from the danger area. Again contact should be made through the bottom half of the ball and with the fist of the inside arm.

If the cross is coming from the right then the punch should be made with the right arm. The upward swinging movement will give you the momentum to get greater distance.

Deflecting

On occasions you will not be able to catch or punch, this may happen if the cross is a deep one to the far post and you may be moving backwards, or the ball may be too high. In this case you should aim to deflect or palm the ball away for a corner. Contact should be made with the arm nearest the goal line.

Deflection is, of course, often the last play in a goalkeeper's repertoire, and has the disadvantage of offering little control of the ball after contact has been made. Timing and commitment are the important elements for success here.

Using the same arrangements as in the previous practice, bring a defender and an attacker in at each end. This will provide opportunities for you to punch, catch and deflect. But only you can make the decision. It will also improve your communications with defenders, to whom you must give clear information as to whether you or they will deal with the cross.

These decisions will improve as you become more experienced. Your confidence will grow the more crosses you have to deal with. Most goalkeepers are happy to deal with crosses around the 'six-yard box', however, Liverpool's Bruce Grobbelaar is renowned for his exploits in the whole of the penalty area. Like most aspects of football, good goalkeeping comes down to confidence. The more you practise, the more competent you will become when situations arise in a game.

DISTRIBUTION

Up to now we have looked at the goalkeeper as a defender and primarily that is his job. However, once you have possession you can set up the next attack with good distribution.

There are two ways in which the goalkeeper can distribute the ball: he can kick it or he can throw it.

Kicking

In the case of kicking, it should be stressed that in the modern game the type of kick is an important part of team strategy. It's important to remember that when the goalkeeper has possession he is in a very privileged position. With the ball in his hands it is very difficult to dispossess him, and he can decide the best course of action he should take on behalf of his team. If you watch games you will see players take up certain positions when the 'keeper has possession and the goalkeeper will automatically throw or kick to specific areas of the pitch.

When the goalkeeper kicks he will use one of two techniques, either (a) the volley kick or (b) the half-volley kick. As we said earlier, team strategy will have a bearing on that choice.

The kick on the volley will take the ball on a high trajectory and is usually favoured by teams who have a couple of big strikers who are good in the air. The half-volley has a lower and faster trajectory and will reach the target a lot quicker than the volley. It is important that you practise both techniques.

When volleying, the ball should be held out in front of you at about waist height. From this position the ball should be dropped. You should strike the ball in front of you, contact being made with the instep through the bottom half of the ball. If you lean back slightly it will give you

SOCCER

Rolling the ball.

more height on the kick. After you have made contact there should be a nice smooth follow-through with the kicking leg.

The initial stages of the volley are the same for the half-volley. The moment of contact however is as the ball touches the ground. You should strike it with your instep. The closer the contact to the midline of the ball the shallower the trajectory.

You can practise using both techniques to kick the ball to a team-mate. Start close together and move apart as you improve. Remember this is a pass, so concentrate on accuracy perhaps reaching your teammate with the first bounce when volleying and possibly straight to him with the half-volley. Strong thigh muscles are helpful in achieving greater distances, but as with most techniques concentration and timing are important factors.

Accuracy is an important aspect of distribution. A long kick up the field will reduce the accuracy level. So, quite often the 'keeper will elect to throw the ball. There are three different techniques for distributing the ball from your hands, the main influence on your choice being the distance you wish to cover.

Throwing

For short distances between 10 and 20yd (3 and 6m) you should opt for the bowling technique, so called because the action is similar to that of a lawn bowler. You should move into a semi-kneeling position with one foot placed well in front of the other. With the ball held with the palm of the hand, it is bowled along the ground. Goalkeepers are often seen playing this type of ball to central defenders positioned just outside the penalty area because it presents the receiver with little or no control problems.

To deliver the ball quicker and over a distance of between 20 and 30yd (6 and 10m) the ball should be thrown from the shoulder. This action is similar to 'putting the shot' in athletics. You should hold the ball with your palm underneath and

GOALKEEPING

behind it and with your elbow bent, the ball should be released from roughly shoulder height as the arm extends. Your stance should be side-ways on and you should lean forward as you release the ball ensuring a direct and low delivery of the ball.

The final technique is to bowl the ball overarm. The action is not dissimilar to that of a bowler in cricket. The ball, once again, is held behind you and brought round in a wide arc. The point of release will determine the height at which the ball will travel; the earlier you release the ball the higher the trajectory. This type of throw can cover distances of up to 40yd (13m).

Again you can practise quite simply by throwing the ball to a team-mate or against a wall. Accuracy is your prime concern but you should vary the distance at which you practise.

We have looked at the individual aspects of the goalkeeper's game, but he is an integral part of the team. All these skills need to blend in with the team arrangements, and communication with fellow team-mates is vital.

From his position the 'keeper can see

SOCCER

GOALKEEPING

Overarm action.

everything. He is the eyes of the defence and he should pass on information, especially when attackers are making blind runs. Confident and positive clear shouts from a 'keeper can avoid many problems and reduce the risk of confusion. Watch the top goalkeepers, they are constantly talking, organising and keeping players on their toes. They dominate their goal area.

Manchester United's Mark Hughes gives a perfect illustration of how to shield the ball from a defender, back to goal.

It's often said that goalkeepers, like wine, get better as they get older. Whereas many footballers' careers finish in their early 30s it's not unusual to find goalkeepers performing at the highest level well into their late 30s. I think in the case of a goalkeeper, knowledge and experience are more valuable than fitness and youth. But it is a thin line that a goalkeeper treads. Games can be won or lost on the strength of his performance.

Practice, dedication and the ability to learn from mistakes are vital elements of a goalkeeper's character. And perhaps a touch of madness helps!

SIX

SET PLAYS & RE-STARTS

It is becoming increasingly difficult to score goals in free play. At the highest level, teams are very evenly matched and more often the game is decided by a goal scored from a set piece. In fact, over 40 per cent of all goals are scored from free kicks, corners, or throw ins. So it is important you spend time working on attacking and defending from set pieces.

FREE · KICKS

A free kick anywhere on the field can be a problem to a defence because the attacker can play the ball without being challenged. It allows the attacking side to place large numbers of players in dangerous areas. Free kicks in the middle third of the pitch are unlikely to produce direct goals; so it is important that the players position themselves in areas which allow direct strikes on goal or create secondary scoring opportunities.

The free kicks in and around the penalty-box bring the biggest rewards and create opportunities for a direct strike at goal. The key element with free-kicks in these areas is to keep them as simple as possible. There is always a danger that teams will dream up a variety of elaborate movements in the hope of confusing the defenders. Usually it will only succeed in confusing your own players and detract from the real purpose – a strike at goal.

We will assume that your team has been awarded a free kick in the area around the D at the edge of the penalty area. The defenders have built a wall in front of you to protect the goal and block attack possibilities. What are the possibilities open to you?

At the simplest level it boils down to the following options: you can play around it, over it, through it, or by-pass it completely.

The choice will largely depend on the strength of your team. If you have a player who is particularly good at swerving or bending shots it would be a crime not to allow him the opportunity to do so at a free kick. Likewise a player who can chip a ball with pace and accuracy should be given the opportunity to take shots at free kicks – such shots which do succeed more than compensate for those which, inevitably, go astray.

England's Bryan Robson, probably one of the best examples of the complete all-round midfield player.

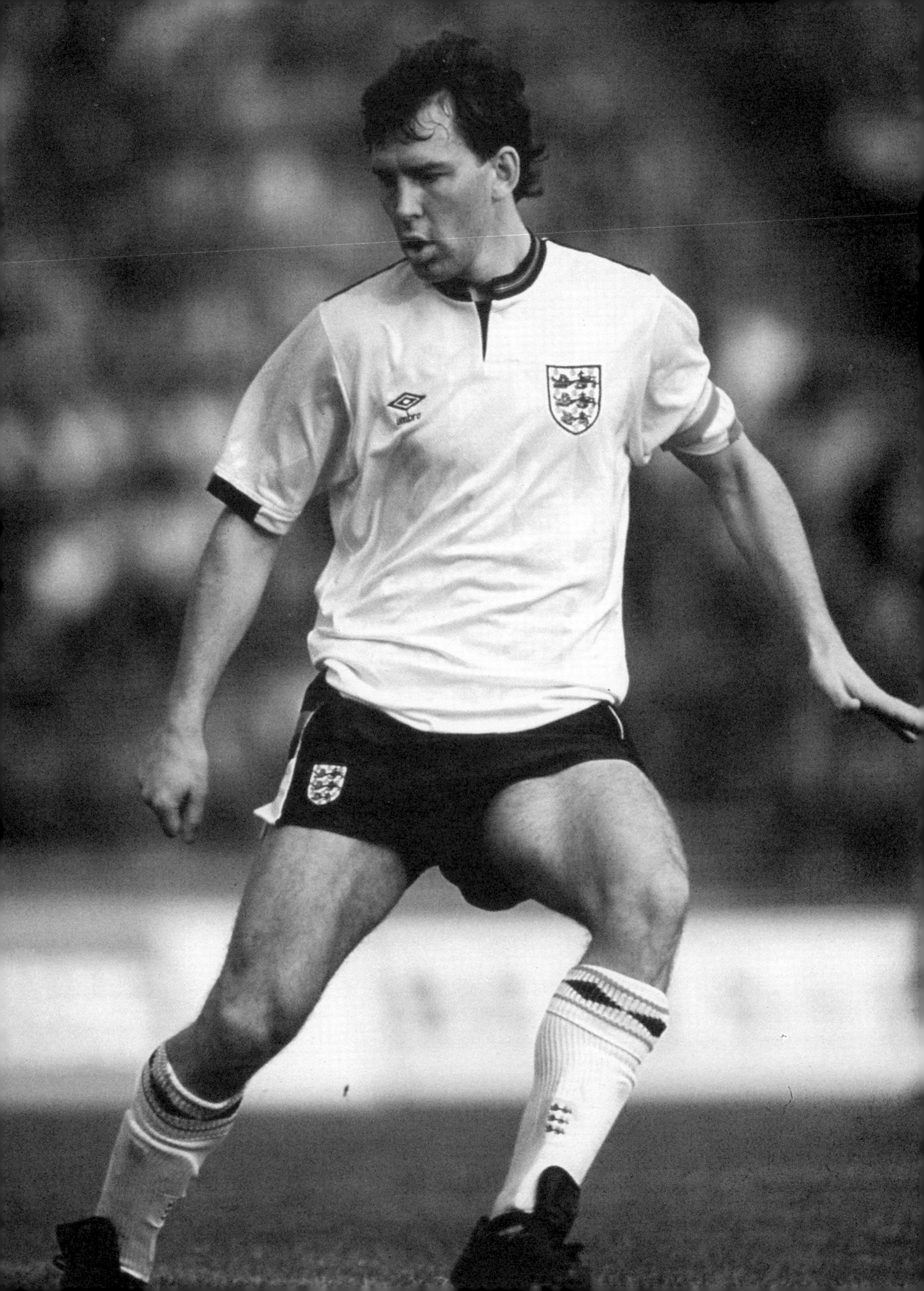

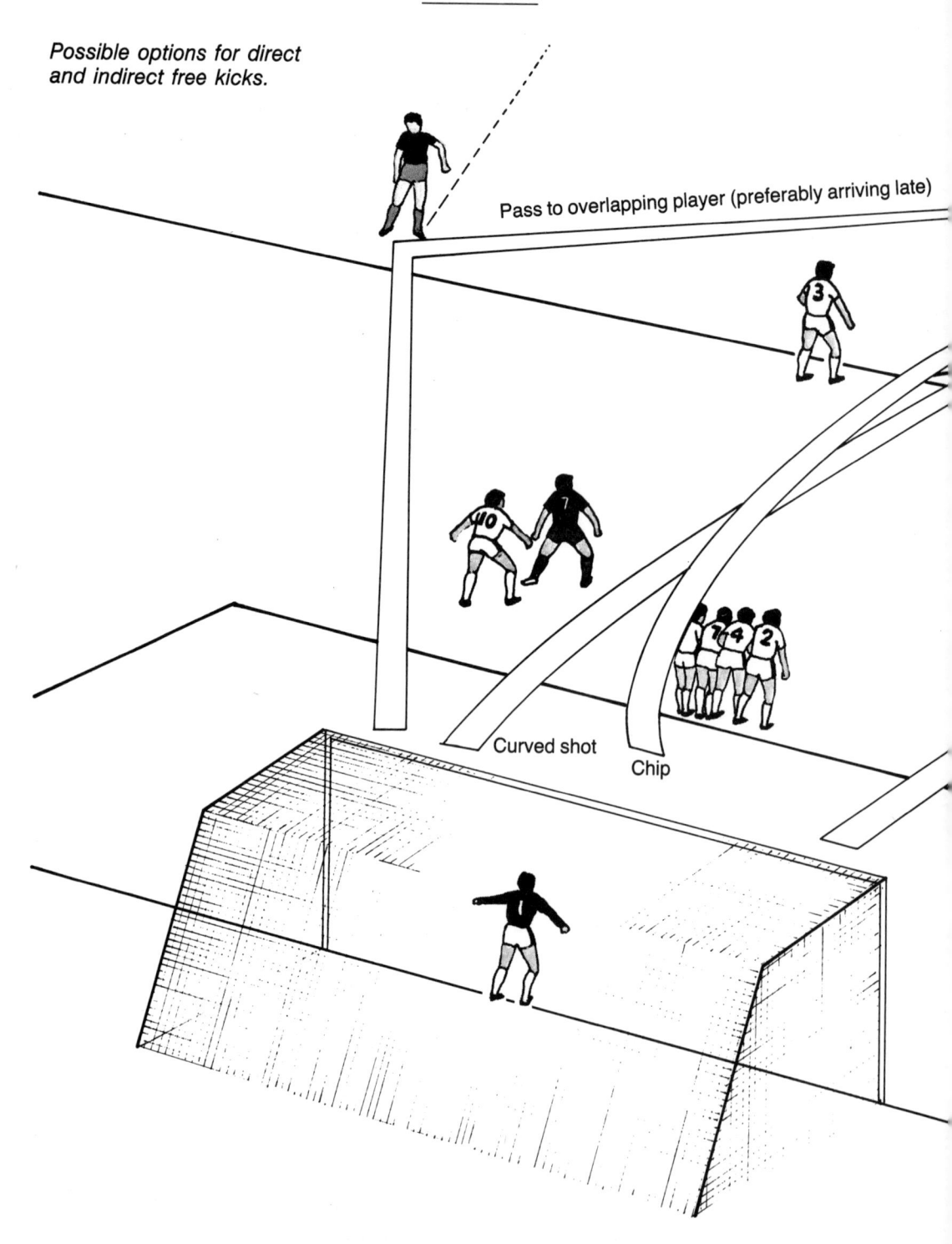

SOCCER

Possible options for direct and indirect free kicks.

Pass to overlapping player (preferably arriving late)

Curved shot

Chip

SET · PLAYS · AND · RE-STARTS

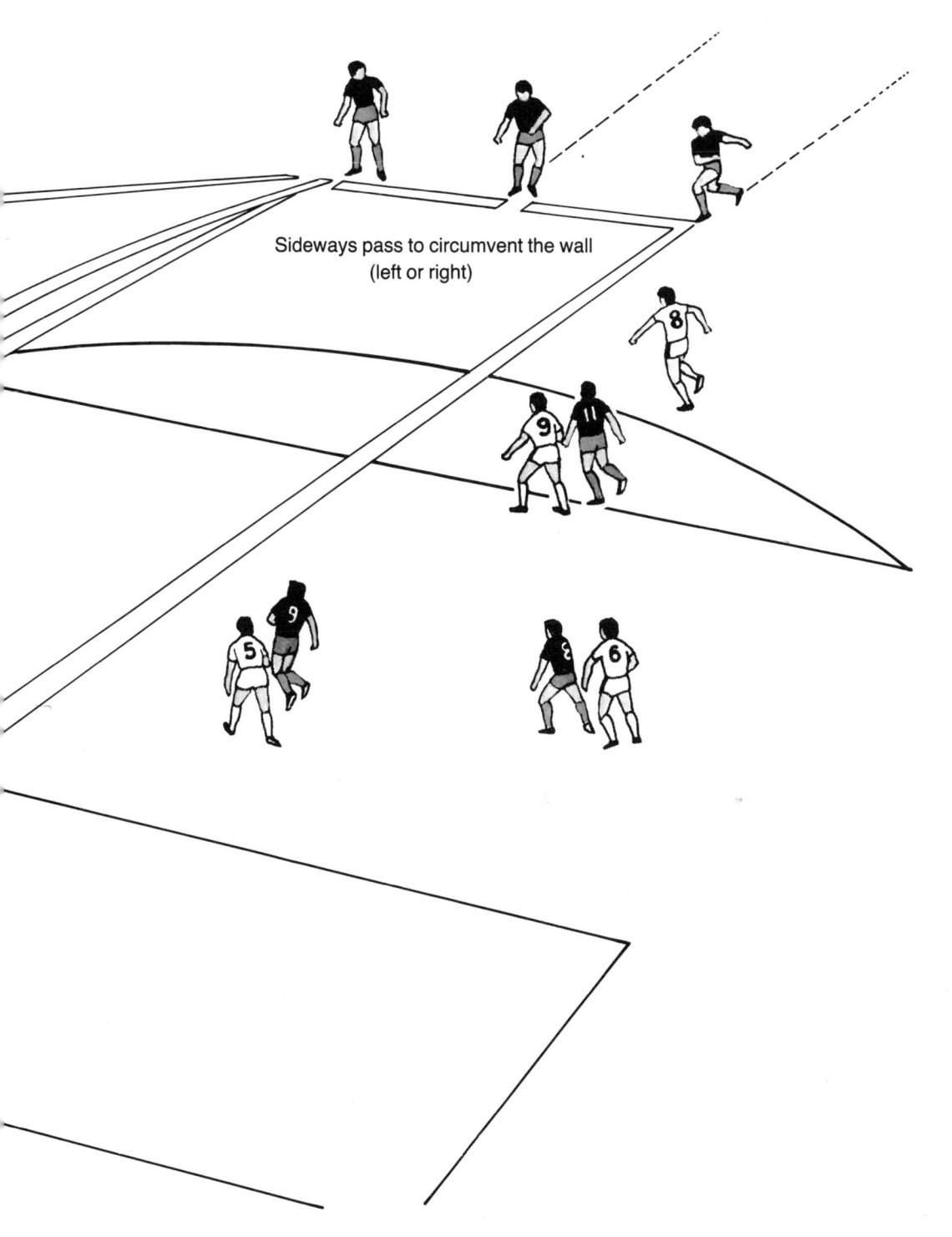

Sideways pass to circumvent the wall
(left or right)

SOCCER

Beating the wall – bending the shot. In this decoy run, the player on the right runs over the ball, and the player on the left follows with a shot.

SET · PLAYS · AND · RE-STARTS

It is important not to rule out the possibility of 'going through the wall'. If you have a player with an exceptionally hard shot then let him have a strike. The general belief is that the wall remains solid, but this sort of player is a test of the wall's character and bravery. Next time you see a free kick in this situation watch what the players do in the wall when the ball is struck. Some will turn or break from the wall. Don't forget that rebounds off the wall can produce secondary scoring chances. So don't dismiss the idea of a direct strike at goal.

Having decided you have a player with a particular strength use him. You can now adopt your team arrangements to suit. You may decide that you are going to bend the ball round the wall. Stick with that idea but try to develop an element of surprise in the hope of misleading the opposition. This can be done quite simply by having two men on the ball, one would be the kicker the other a decoy. The aim of the decoy player is to unsight or distract the goalkeeper and defenders. He does this simply by running over the ball. The follow up shot should be instant for the movement of the other player will only distract or obscure for a split second, but that is long enough for a goal to be scored.

Another simple development of this theme is to place a couple of your own players on the end of the defensive wall. The goalkeeper will line up his wall to cover one side of his goal then position himself to cover the opposite side. The two players should position themselves on the end of the wall covered by the goalkeeper.

Extra attackers on the end of the wall obscure the goalkeeper's view, and the kick is bent around the outside of the wall.

SOCCER

In this position the players are obscuring the goalkeeper's view of the ball. They should remain in this position until the moment the ball is struck, when they should break away from the wall with the outside player turning to the right, and the inside player to the left. Once again the goalkeeper's view of the ball is obscured and he has the added distraction of the players' movements.

Teams will have several variations for free kicks. Many will revolve around the movements of players rather than too many touches on the ball.

Obviously the more touches on the ball, the more chances there are for errors. So don't waste the chance to have a direct strike at goal especially if you have a player who can bend, drive, or chip a ball with a good degree of accuracy.

The same applies with indirect free kicks. In these situations you have to pass the ball. But don't use two passes when one will do.

Assuming the free kick is in the same position as before, then the positioning of players can be the same as for the direct free kick. The arrangements will help disguise the real intention, which is now the square pass.

Timing is an important factor; the ball can be played square into space either side of the wall. The pass should coincide with the forward runs of players who have been positioned behind the ball. In both instances the players should be encouraged to shoot first time at the goal.

However, sometimes the ball played outside the wall may create a difficult shooting angle, in which case the ball should be driven across the face of the goal. This will create opportunities for incoming forwards.

No matter whether the free kick is in front of goal or in a wide position, your first thought should be to get a strike on goal with the least number of touches of the ball.

As we have said, the award of a free kick in and around the penalty box creates a feeling of excitement and anticipation for the attacking side. For the defending side it can be an anxious time which can create confusion and sometimes panic. These problems can be eased if players have practised the defensive arrangements and have good individual discipline and concentration.

Assume again a direct free kick has been awarded in the 'D' on the edge of the penalty box and this time you are defending. Your first reaction should be to position yourself 10yds (9m) away from the ball in line between the ball and your own goal. It's important for players to react immediately a free kick is awarded. So many players lose concentration when the game is stopped and before they know it the ball is in the back of the net. So make sure you and your team-mates react the moment the kick is awarded.

The defensive wall

Having prevented a quick strike on goal we now embark on an operation which is peculiar to football. The building of a defensive wall.

This should not be regarded as a haphazard operation but one that requires planning and organisation and a good deal of bravery from the players selected to be positioned in the wall.

The number of players required to make up the wall will vary depending on the position of the free kick. A kick from a central position will require 4/5 players with the number decreasing as kicks move to wider positions.

Mexico's Hugo Sanchez, renowned for his overhead kicks when shooting for goal, seen here performing his equally famous somersault when he has scored.

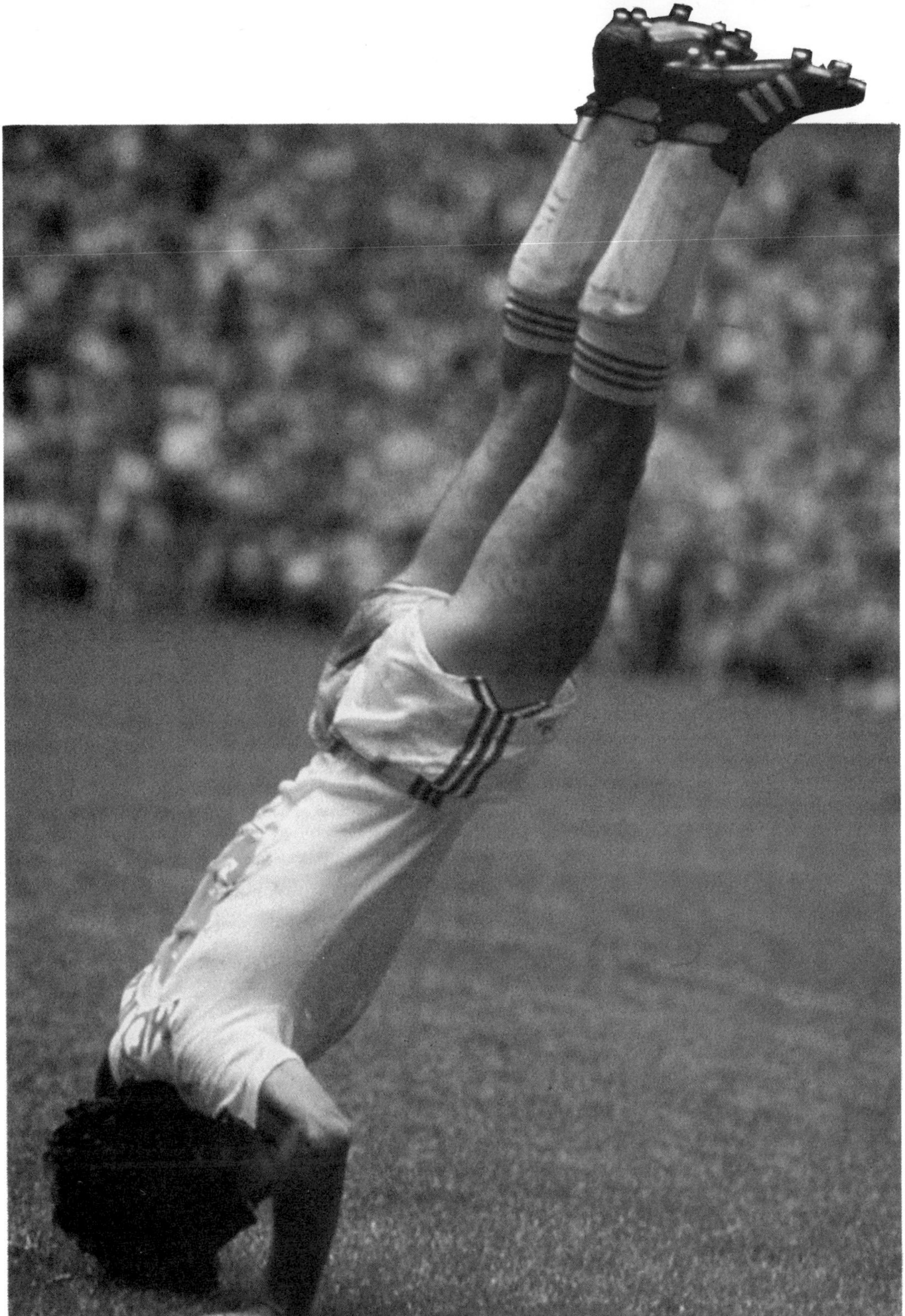

SOCCER

It is generally thought that the goalkeeper takes the responsibility for lining up the wall, but many teams have an outfield player standing behind the ball doing the lining-up. This reduces the chance of the opposition having a quick strike while the goalkeeper is busy organising the wall.

Ideally, the goalkeeper needs to be positioned near the centre of his goal where he can see the ball. He should not be directly behind the defensive wall but to one side of it. It is his decision which side of the goal the wall will defend and which side he will defend.

Once this has been decided a player should be positioned to defend on the end of the wall, his position being just outside the line between the ball and the post. This will make it difficult for a shot to be bent around the wall. The rest of the players then take up their positions off him. The tallest player should be positioned on the outside of the wall, with the wall reducing in size as it moves inside. This will obviously force the kicker to put extra height on the kick should he choose to go round the outside – height that could be the difference between the ball going under or over the bar.

The players should know who are required for 'wall-building duties' in advance. Generally that should not include traditional defenders. They should take up positions where the real defending has to be done. The players in the wall have to be prepared to hold their ground. They should be close together and prevent the kicker from having clear sight of his target – the goal.

Now that the players in the wall know their roles they should move into their respective positions whenever a free kick is awarded around the penalty box, with the goalkeeper deciding upon the number required to make the wall.

With up to five players involved in the wall your opposition will have an obvious numerical advantage, so it is important that all players of the defending team get behind the ball. In these situations players will sometimes mark man-for-man or mark areas, like the far post, which are threatened by incoming players.

In the case of an indirect free kick it is as well to have a player on the inside of the wall whose job is to charge down the short pass to the side.

Defending against free kicks is never easy, but a lot of the problems will be reduced with good organising and planning. Players will feel that little bit more secure in the knowledge that they and everyone else understand their role, reducing the feeling of panic. And if the danger is cleared confidence will grow.

SET · PLAYS · AND · RE-STARTS

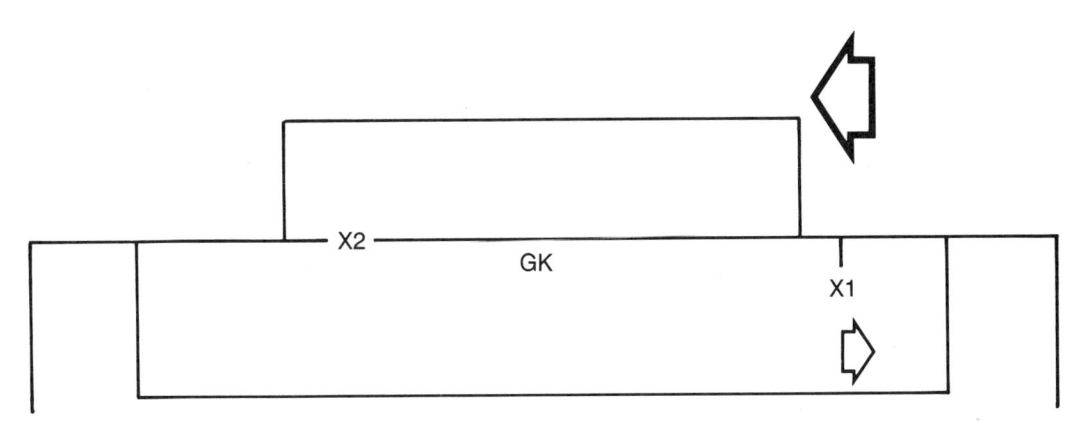

X1 defends just in front of the near post; the goalkeeper positions himself centrally in the goal, and X2 positions himself inside the far post.

CORNERS

The principles applied to defending at free kicks generally apply to defending at corners. Good organization, discipline and concentration are the foundations of the successful defensive unit.

Again, the goalkeeper has a major role to play, both as an organiser and in a practical sense. He should be positioned in the middle of his goal where he can move quickly to balls played to both the near and far posts. He should adopt a side-on position to help him organise and increase his own awareness of what is happening around him.

It is customary to place a defender close to each post. The choice of players

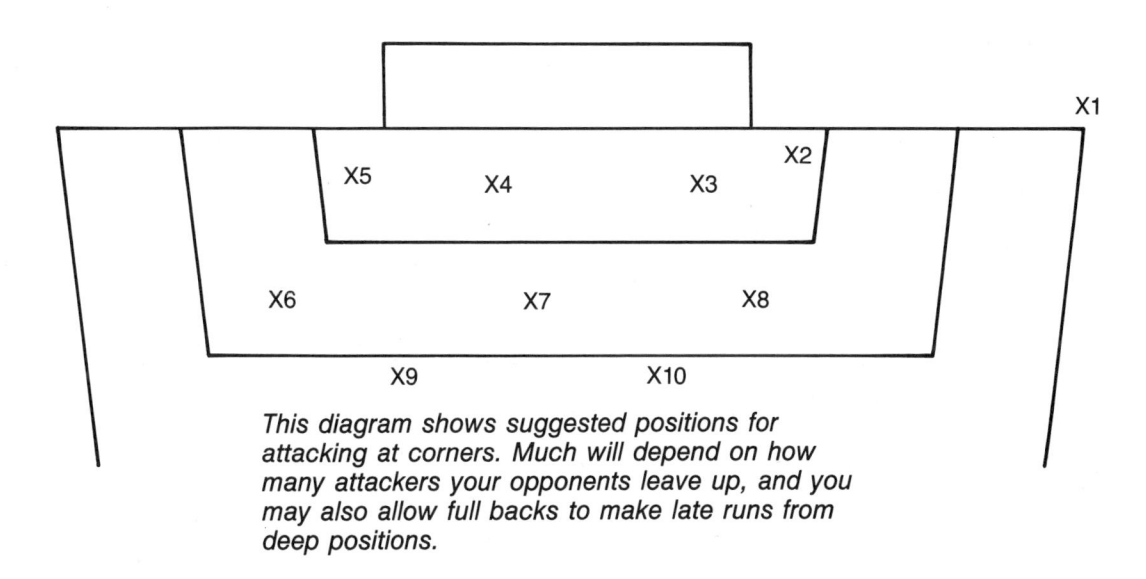

This diagram shows suggested positions for attacking at corners. Much will depend on how many attackers your opponents leave up, and you may also allow full backs to make late runs from deep positions.

· 95 ·

SOCCER

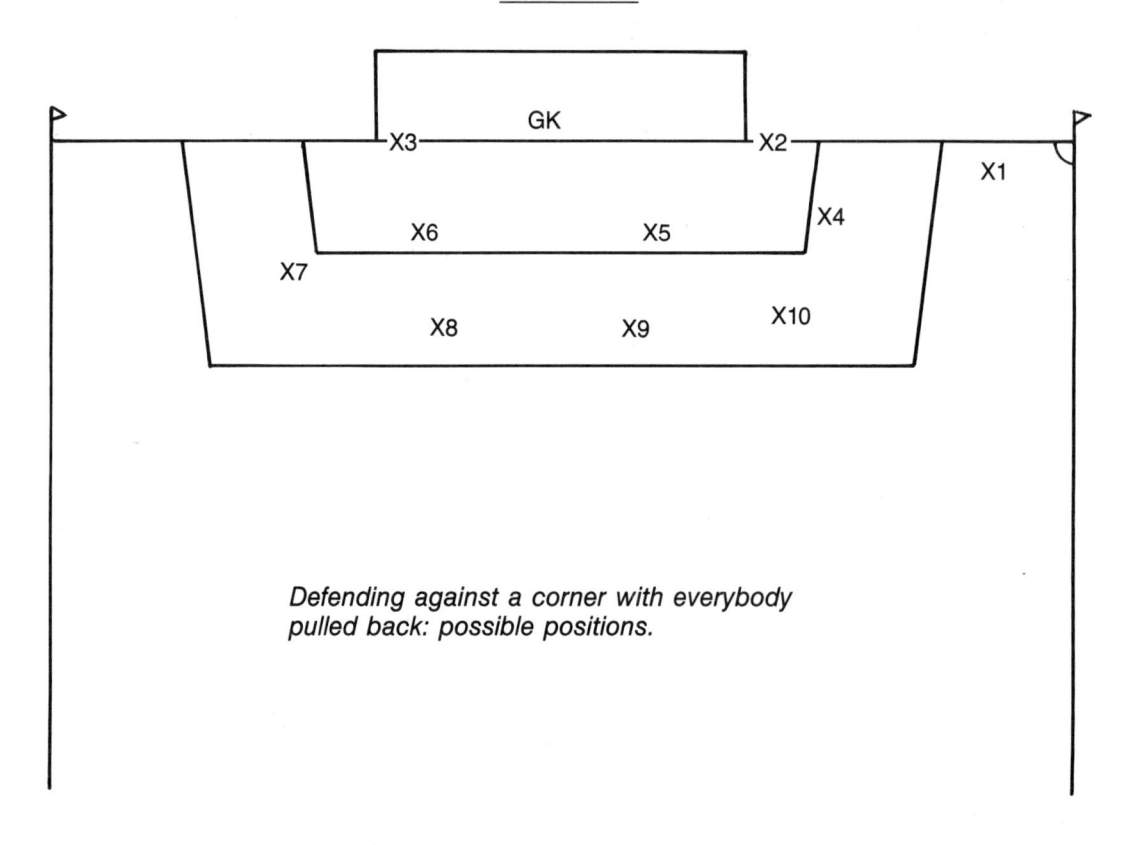

Defending against a corner with everybody pulled back: possible positions.

to mark the post should be made before the game starts. In most cases it is the full backs who occupy these positions. But if one full back is particularly tall then he would be better utilized marking a tall attacker in the penalty area. This is where it comes down to pre-planning for these set pieces.

The player defending the near post should take up a position just in front of the post and should concern himself with attacking balls played into the space in front of him. The player defending the far post should be inside the post and take up a stance similar to the goalkeeper's, allowing him to see the ball and observe the movements of opponents beyond the far post. Some teams also place a player 10yd (10m) in front of the kick taken.

From this position he will be able to affect the delivery and technique of the kicker and also reduce the possibilities of short corners.

Defending teams will again pull most of their players back, and they will concentrate on the areas around the six yard box. The attackers, on the other hand will be concerned with the areas between the six yard and 18-yard lines.

Each defender should know his role and be prepared to compete for a ball played into his specific area. The area around the six yard box is the most vulnerable. A player should cover the front of the box and be ready to attack balls played to the near post. Other defenders can be placed along the six yard line. In line with these players, but about 12yd (11m) out, three

SET · PLAYS · AND · RE-STARTS

other players can be positioned allowing them to attack balls played wider.

These are only rough guidelines, but you will generally find that attackers will take up positions ready to attack these areas. The important thing is to attack the ball and compete for it until it has been cleared from the penalty area.

A goalkeeper who is good at handling crosses can influence the type of corners taken by the attacking team. If he dominates the six yard box and his handling is good he may force the attacking side to swing the corners away from him, which eases the pressure on the defence.

Once the ball is cleared the defence should move out quickly together as a complete unit, closing down on the player in possession and perhaps catching opponents offside should the ball be played back quickly.

Inswinging corner

As with free kicks, several variations can be used when taking a corner kick. Again the choice will depend on the strengths of your team. However, the most important thing is the quality and accuracy of the kicker. It is no use making your team arrangements, positioning your players in a particular area, only to find that your kicker cannot deliver the ball.

Probably the most difficult corner to defend is the in-swinger or ball played to the near post. The delivery is made easier if you have a left-footed player deliver the ball from the right and vice versa.

For this type of cross the six yard box is very much the target area for both the attacking and defending team. Usually the attacking team will position a tall player between the near post and the edge of the six yard box. Some teams use two players. The accuracy of the kicker now becomes crucial. He needs to deliver a ball that has pace and is at a height

which enables the player to flick the ball on with his head. While it is unlikely the attacker will score from this position (although it is not impossible), his aim is to flick the ball on to one or two team mates positioned behind him in a central position in front of the goal. They are the ones who should then capitalise on the flick.

There are variations on this theme. Rather than flick the ball on, he could deflect it into a wider position between the penalty spot and the 18 yard line or he could come down the line and play a short corner, with the ball delivered deep.

SOCCER

Inswinging corner to the near post. A left-footed player is taking the kick. Attackers are grouped around the near post.

Outswinging corner

Alternatively, you could use a deeper ball or outswinging corner. The kicker responsible for this sort of kick should be a right-footed player if the kick is from the right, or vice versa if it is from the left. Team arrangements have to take into account that the ball will be delivered to the area of the far post.

If the kicker has a good technique then the ball driven into the near post area swinging away from the goal is ideal for an in rushing player.

A short corner can often disturb defenders. The point of attack is suddenly changed and it requires defenders making quick decisions outside the pre-planned arrangements.

The ball laid back down the line to an oncoming full back is a simple short corner. From this position he can run with the ball. Alternatively, he can cross the ball first time, which can catch defending teams unaware because they have to make quick adjustments in relation to the line and trajectory of the ball.

It is important that attackers know what kind of corner the kicker is going to deliver. It is no sense the attacking unit being geared up for a near-post ball when

SET · PLAYS · AND · RE-STARTS

the kicker plays an outswinger. They should be fully aware of the type of kick to expect. This is often simply done by the kicker giving a pre-arranged signal to his attackers. After that it is up to him to deliver an accurate kick.

THROW-INS

Finally, a set play that many players tend to ignore is the throw-in. In any game, irrespective of its level, your team can expect to receive more throw-ins than any other type of set play so it is worth devoting a little bit of thought to team arrangements, especially when the throws are in range of the 18 yard box.

If you have a player who can throw the ball a long distance he should be utilised for throws that are close to the 18-yard box.

The quality of the throw is important. It should have pace and be aimed at the head of a player positioned in an area around the near post. This player should look to deflect or flick the ball on, depending on the angle from which the ball is delivered. However, he should not rule out the possibility of scoring himself.

Throw-ins in other areas of the field may not produce such instant results. But if their importance is appreciated they can be a vital source of goalscoring opportunities. The player with the ball should be looking to take the throw quickly and accurately and in attacking situations should be aiming to throw the ball into the space behind defenders.

Defending against the long throw should take on the same importance as defending at corners. It is a threat on your goal so concentration and the correct attitude are vital. Again the goalkeeper should command his six-yard box and be competitive and confident in the air. Depending upon the quality of the throw, it is often advantageous for the defending team to position a player in front of the attacker on the near post. This is because the thrower will usually direct the throw at about head height. A defender in front may be able to block this.

SOCCER

SET · PLAYS · AND · RE-STARTS

When the ball goes out of play in other less dangerous areas of the pitch, defenders often look upon it as a chance to 'take a breather'. This is fatal. It is often during the brief momentary lack of concentration that the attacking team makes a breakaway. No matter where the ball goes out of play, be alert and ready to defend, and keep your eye on any players who are making a run ready to receive the throw.

As we said, more than 40 per cent of goals are scored from set plays so it is very important that defenders and attackers spend time working on these areas of their game. Like the individual techniques, the more you practise set plays the better you and your team will become. At the same time understanding and confidence will grow.

Planning, organization, good discipline, and concentration are the key elements of defending and attacking at any set play, with a good quality delivery completing the list of qualities for attacking play.

Ian Rush celebrates a goal for Liverpool, from close range, emphasizing the importance of secondary goal-scoring chances.

SEVEN

FITNESS TRAINING FOR SOCCER

To be successful and enjoy any sport, it is important to have good basic skills and technique, and vital that you are fit enough to perform those skills. In football you have to gear your fitness to at least 90 minutes playing time.

At a very early age youngsters have a natural fitness. They have an abundance of energy and spend lots of their time running, jumping and playing games. But the increased popularity of television and computers in recent years has brought a decline in physical activities. As youngsters become teenagers their fitness can be destroyed completely by over-indulgence.

It is important that young players look after their health and personal fitness. They need to prepare their bodies correctly if they are to make the grade in top class football.

The game of football puts many different demands on the body but your preparation can be placed under four main headings: flexibility, stamina, strength and speed.

We will look at the various ways of improving your fitness, coupled with a mental determination to want to improve. Follow these guidelines and you should achieve a good standard of football fitness.

FLEXIBILITY

Flexibility refers to the suppleness and mobility of the body which provides footballers with good balance and the ability to perform intricate movements, such as body swerves, smoothly.

Flexibility exercises involve stretching different muscles and should be performed before and after every training session.

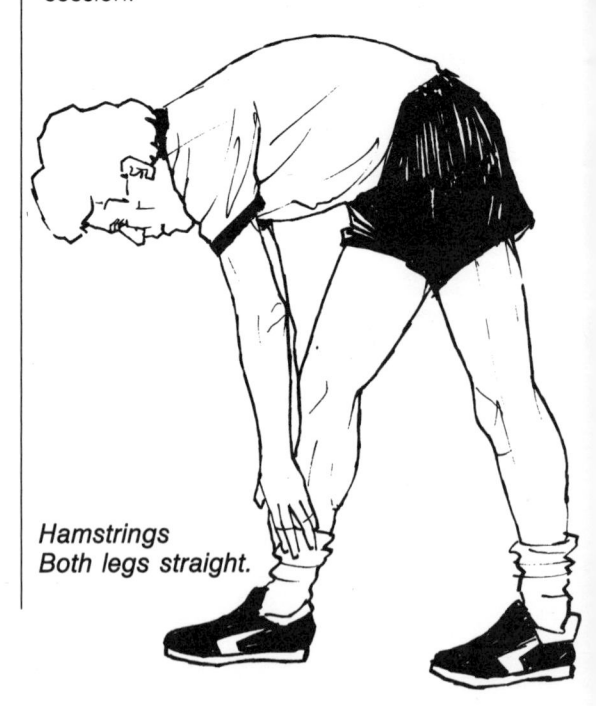

Hamstrings
Both legs straight.

FITNESS · TRAINING · FOR · SOCCER

Not only will these exercises improve flexibility, but they warm-up and loosen-up muscles before they are subjected to a vigorous training session.

Hamstring

To loosen up the hamstring stand straight, place the heel of your right foot directly in front of your left foot. Keeping your legs straight, slowly ease your hands down and try to touch in front of your right foot. When you feel you are fully stretched hold that position for five seconds. Repeat the process with your left leg at the front.

Calf

For loosening up the calf bend your right leg in front of you, and stretch your other leg directly behind you. Ensure your rear leg is straight and the heel is flat on the floor. Slowly push your chest towards your front leg. When you feel fully stretched hold the position for five seconds, relax, and repeat the process with your other leg in front of you.

Groin and inside leg

A similar position as for the calf stretch should be adopted when loosening up the groin or inside leg. This time, however, your rear leg should be at 90° to your front foot so the inside of your foot is flat on the floor. Slowly push your chest towards your front leg and, when you feel fully stretched, hold the position for five seconds, relax and repeat on the other leg.

Calf
Both feet in line.
Rear leg straight.
Rear heel on floor.

Abductors
Front foot straight.
Rear leg straight.
Rear foot at 90°.

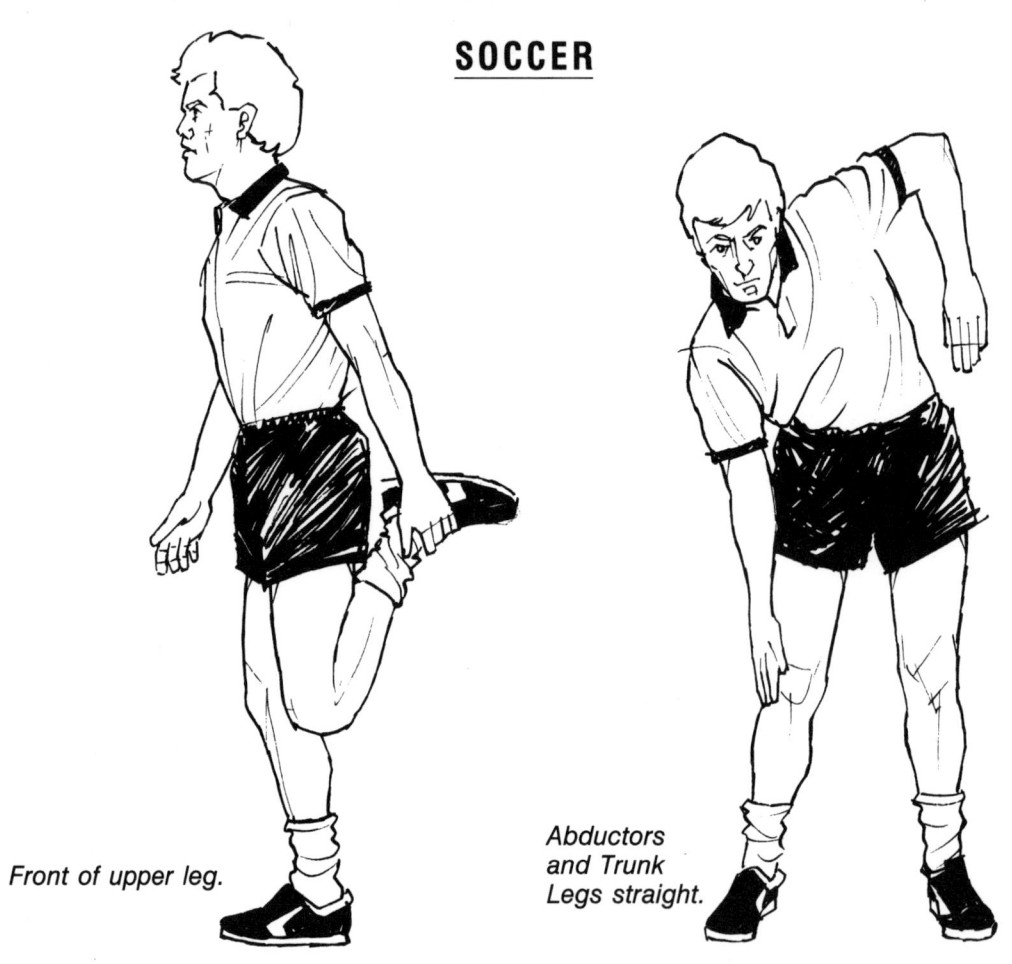

SOCCER

Front of upper leg.

Abductors and Trunk Legs straight.

Quadriceps

The quadraceps exercise should be carried out by standing upright. Lift and bend your leg behind you; clasp your ankle, keep the leg close to the standing leg, not out on an angle. While pulling your foot into your back try pushing to the floor and hold the position for five seconds, relax, and then repeat on the other leg.

Middle body

To exercise the middle body stand upright with your legs about 18in (40cm) apart and clasp your hands behind your head. Keep your legs straight and flat on the floor, push your left elbow as far behind you as possible, then repeat on the right hand side.

Maintaining the same position, bend forward and try to touch the inside of your left knee with your right elbow. Stand up straight and touch the inside of your right knee with your left elbow.

Keeping your upper body straight, and legs slightly apart, put your hands by your sides and push your right hand past your right knee, return to the upright position and repeat on the left hand side.

Arms and shoulders

To help get your arms and shoulders supple, stand upright with your legs slightly apart; raise your right arm and rotate it with a bowling action. Then repeat

FITNESS · TRAINING · FOR · SOCCER

Arms and Shoulders
Full circle movement.

Neck Roll
Keep the rest of the body fixed.

the same action in the opposite direction. The same action is repeated with the left arm.

Neck

And finally an exercise for the neck, an area many players neglect. Stand upright with your legs slightly apart and firmly on the floor. Start with your chin on your chest and rotate your head towards your right shoulder, roll it to the back on to your left shoulder and finish with your chin back on your chest. Repeat the exercise in the opposite direction.

These are just a few examples of exercises that will improve not only your flexibility but your performance and help to prevent injuries such as strains and pulled muscles.

SOCCER

FITNESS · TRAINING · FOR · SOCCER

STAMINA

The next two aspects of training, strength and stamina, provide the footballer with endurance, a vital quality which enables him to compete during 90 minutes of football.

Improving strength will enable you to tackle harder, kick further and jump higher, while regular stamina work will allow you to run with and without the ball for 90 minutes virtually non-stop.

Running and strength exercises can be combined to provide a balanced and regular training schedule. We will look at some ideas for training schedules and a way of improving strength.

Achieving a good level of stamina means running. To some players this is a hardship, but to others it comes easy and they actually enjoy running. To reach the top level it has to be done and it requires a strong mental attitude.

When embarking on any training programme, you should start off slowly and gradually build up. Bear in mind, the earlier you start, the sounder your base level of stamina will be.

At school, youngsters may have an opportunity to run two or three days a week, or enjoy a couple of training sessions with a local club. Quite often this is not enough and the player(s) will have to do extra work on their own. This will involve running at the local park or on the open roads, but the quality of the runs is more important than the distance covered. It is better running four to five miles, varying your pace, than plodding around a ten mile circuit. Lamp-posts, trees, buildings etc., can provide useful targets for varying your pace. Sprinting between

England's Bryan Robson and Steve McMahon in training. Good levels of fitness are vital, allowing players to perform to the best of their ability.

SOCCER

one set of trees whilst jogging to the next set is a good idea. Try to include running up hills or if possible on sand.

Playing football, both 11- and 5-a-side, regularly, is a more enjoyable way of building up stamina, but again a good mental approach is vital. If you tell yourself you will not stand still during a game and will keep moving no matter where the play is then it shows you have the right attitude. A couple of games of 5-a-side a week, or 7-a-side on a full sized pitch, are great assets to any stamina-building programme.

Working with a ball both as individuals and as a group should not be neglected. Running 40 yards (35m) with the ball, having a shot at goal, returning for another ball and repeating the run is hard work, but you can also find it enjoyable. Keeping the ball in the air with the foot, thigh and head, or dribbling around a slalom course, may be very demanding, but they are good stamina-building exercises.

As you can see, with a little bit of imagination, building up your stamina need not be tedious and boring. It can actually be fun. But it is down to you to show the right attitude.

STRENGTH

The development of good all-round body strength is an important part of any sportsman's training. However, in addition to all-round body strength you need to concentrate on the particular muscle areas which will improve your performance over 90 minutes of play.

The key area for a footballer is his legs and lower body. Strengthening these will enable you to kick further, tackle harder and jump higher. We will now look at a number of exercises aimed at improving the strength of your legs.

Skipping

Usually related to boxers, but as it helps them to last 12 rounds, so it will help you to last 90 minutes. Try straightforward skipping, jumping with both feet, then alternate from one foot to another.

Step-ups

Using a bench or chair, stand in front of it and place your left foot onto it. Bring your right foot alongside so you are standing upright. Repeat the exercise using your right foot first. Usually this is done in sets; 20 step-ups per set.

Step-ups: step completely on and off the bench

FITNESS · TRAINING · FOR · SOCCER

Astride jumps on a bench.

Stride jumps

Using a bench, place your feet either side of it and jump upwards bringing your feet together so you land on the bench. Jump off the bench with feet astride. The exercise should be repeated quickly, again in sets of 20.

Similar exercises can be done using a ball. With the ball in front of you, lightly step on with the left foot, then on with the right. You will be able to build up a steady rhythm.

The stride jumps are again similar, with the feet lightly touching the top of the ball when raised.

Squat thrusts

Take up a position as if you were going to do press-ups, with your legs outstretched behind you and with your hands flat on the floor, shoulder-width apart. Bring your knees up so they touch just behind your elbows and then push them back out straight behind you. At speed do a set of 20.

Squat Thrusts

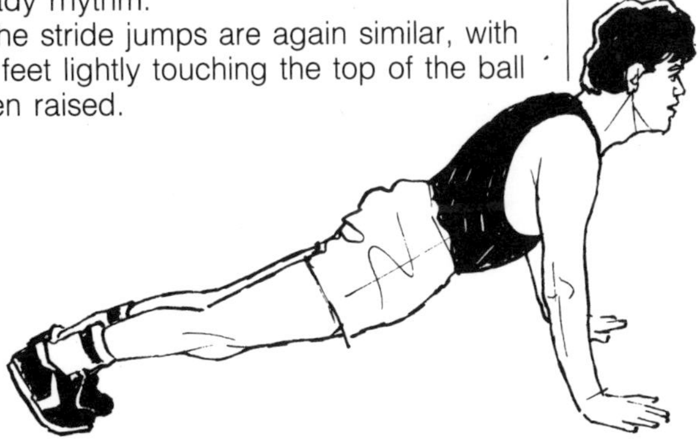

SOCCER

Diagonal sit-ups with knees bent

Sit-ups

Sit-ups are designed to develop the upper body. Begin by lying on your back and place your hands in front of your thighs. Raise your shoulders so your hands move down your thighs and touch your knees. Return to rest slowly, and repeat in sets of 10.

As you become stronger progress by placing your hands behind your head, bend your right arm towards your left knee, touching it with your right elbow. Repeat the exercise with the right leg and left elbow.

Running with the ball is a big feature of the European game, illustrated here by Frank Rijkaard of Holland.

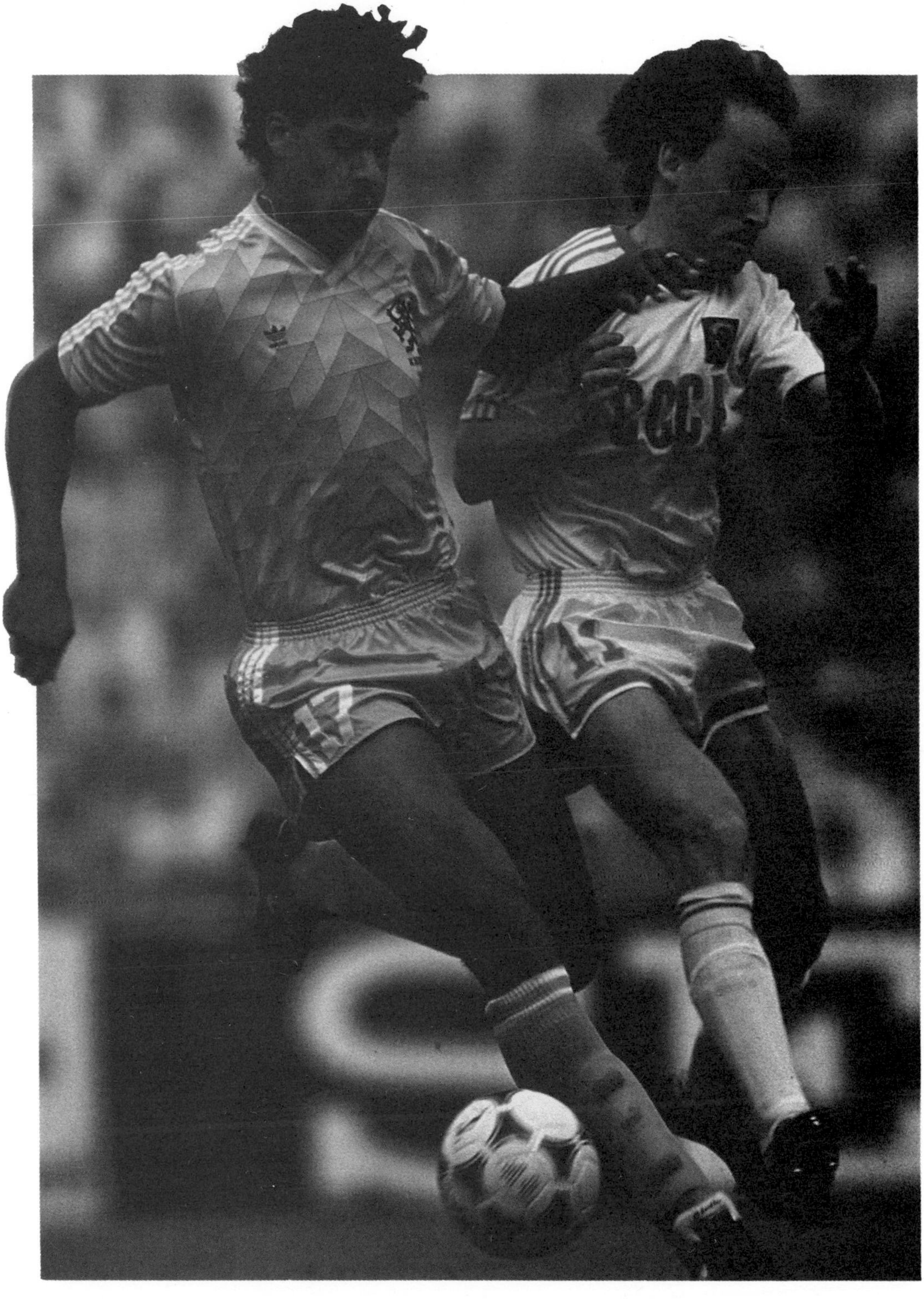

SOCCER

EXERCISES

Straight arm swings

Sit-ups

Press-ups

Trunk curls

Shuttle-runs (set of four)

FITNESS · TRAINING · FOR · SOCCER

Step-ups

Stride-jumps

Squat thrusts

Star-jumps

SOCCER

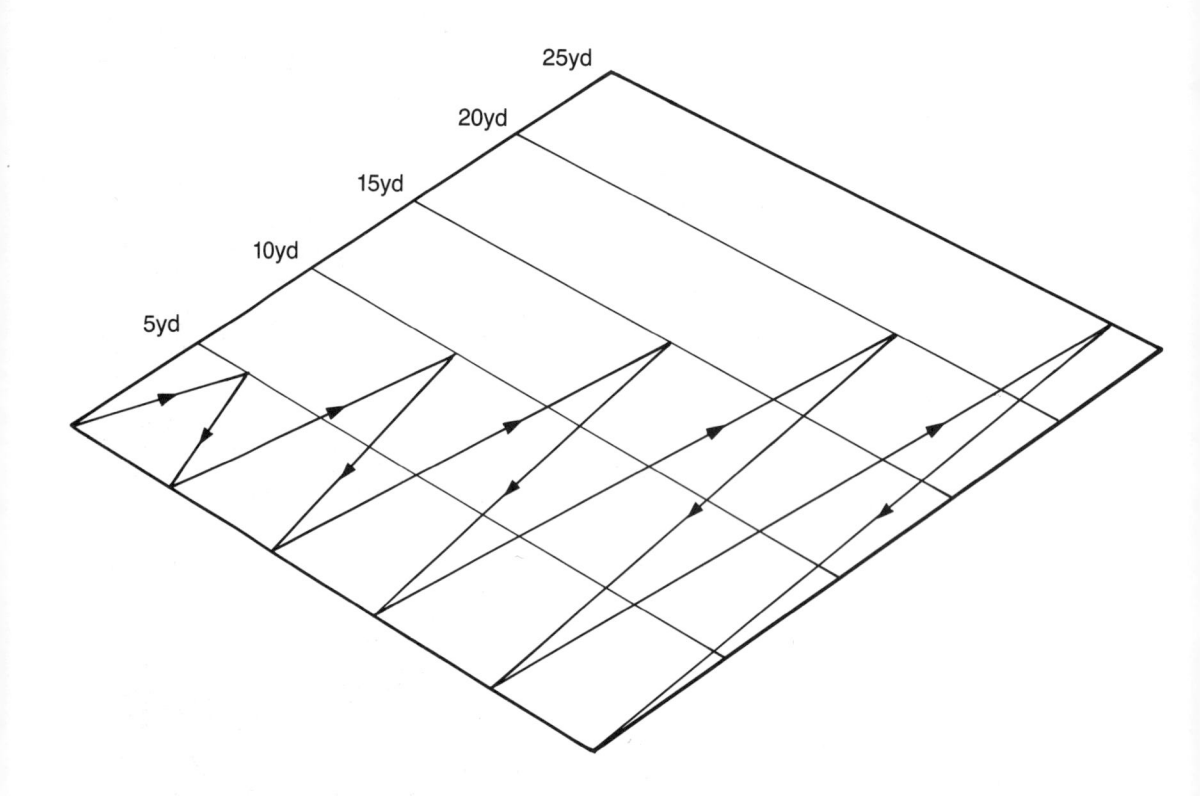

The most popular form of fitness training is Shuttle Running, it is simple to organize and constitutes most types of runs footballers have to make in terms of distance. In the above example players run a total of 150 yd by completing the course as shown. They should set out to complete the course in 35 seconds, then rest for 35 seconds before going again, thus they cover 150 yd in sprints of 10, 20, 30, 40 and 50 yd.

Players should not neglect their upper-body, it needs to be strong to sustain bodily contact. Sprinting also depends as much on the arms as the legs, and strength around the shoulders, chest and arms also improves sprinting power.

This strength is usually gained by weight training. Individual weights such as barbells and dumbbells can be used but a popular method now is the use of multi-gyms. These machines offer the user the opportunity to strengthen all parts of the body within a limited space. Whatever your choice, expert advice should be taken before using any weights.

A good way of building all-round strength and stamina is to combine various exercises into a circuit like the one shown.

Again start off slowly. Do each exercise

FITNESS · TRAINING · FOR · SOCCER

The 'Dutch Master' Johan Cruyff, remembered for his famous 'Cruyff Turn'.

SOCCER

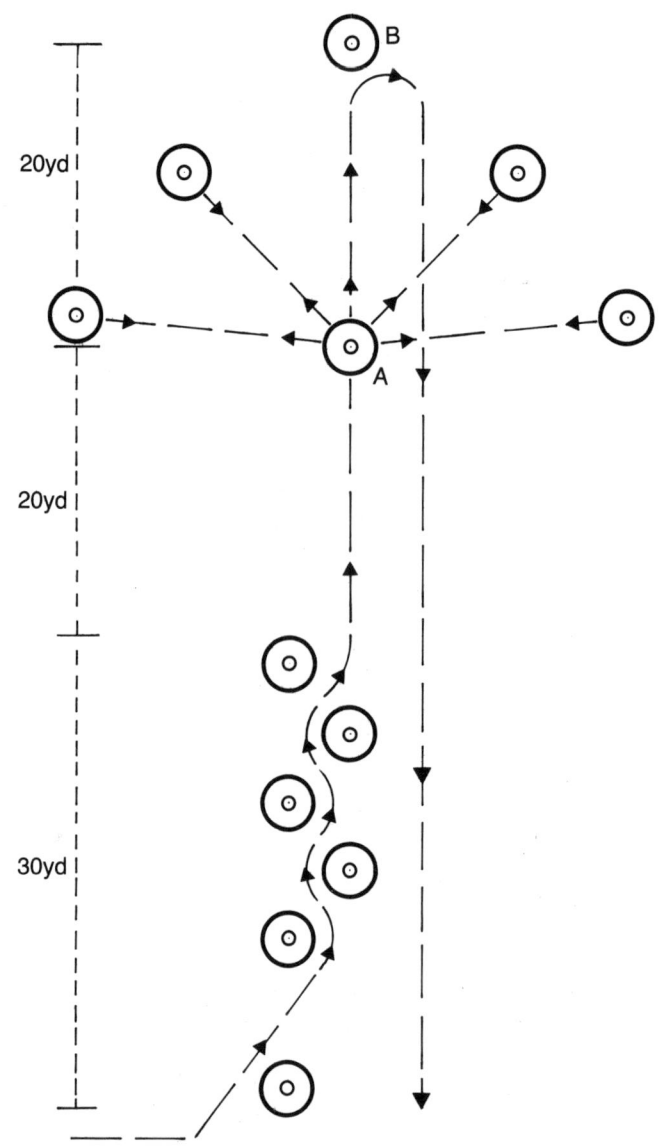

Player sprints through first set of cones and onto cone 'A'; from there he sprints to all outer cones finishing with cone B and returning to the start position. There are numerous variations to this exercise; here are two:

a) *Two teams at the start, players competing against each other, through the circuit to cone 'A' together they complete the fan with one player sprinting to the cone on the far right, the other to the left.*

b) *Using a ball, player sprints through the first set of cones with the ball; leaves it at cone 'A'; completes a series of sprints; returns to start with ball through first set of cones again.*

FITNESS · TRAINING · FOR · SOCCER

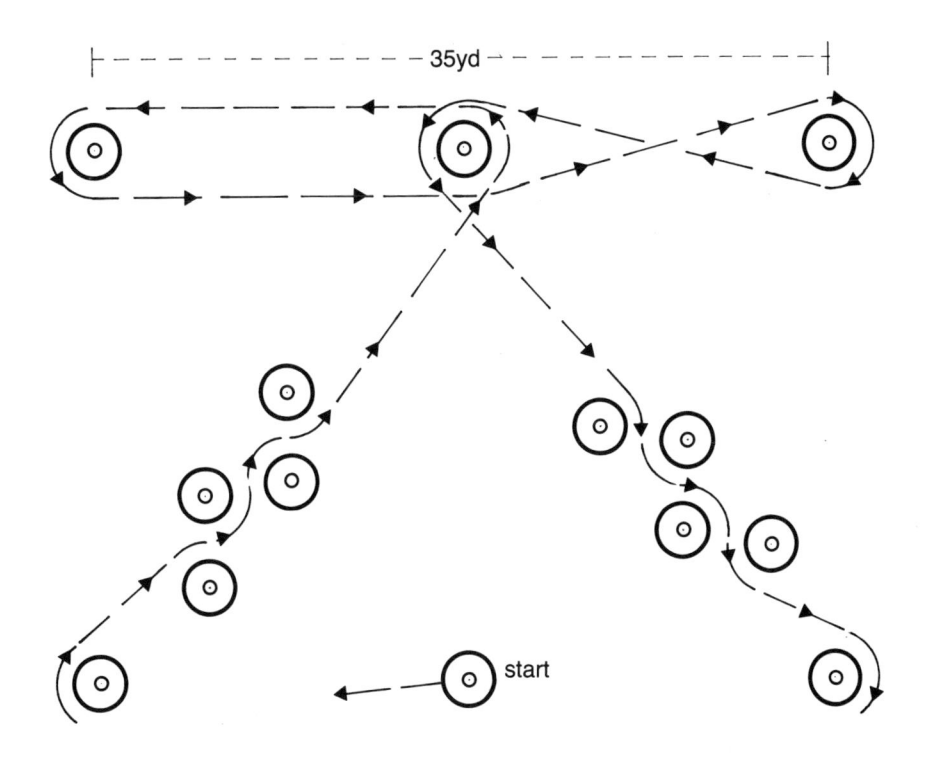

Known to the players as the 'Bermuda Triangle', the circuit is completed as follows:

a) Two teams at the start, players competing against each other. The players sprint in opposite directions, rounding first cone and completing full circuit.

b) Complete or part circuits with a ball, racing against each other (as above), or a solo run against the clock.

for 30 seconds with a one-minute rest period between each. As you get fitter increase the time you exercise and reduce your rest period.

All the foregoing are just a few of the numerous exercises for the legs. But remember; when attempting any exercise you should start slowly and build up gradually. Working too hard, or trying to get fit too quickly, brings with it the serious risk of injury, as some well-known professionals have found to their cost. Always keep within the limits recommended by experts.

SPEED

Speed is not just a question of being fast, it is that explosive burst that makes it look as though the other player is 'standing still'. Quickness off the mark, the ability to turn quickly and sprint in another direction are all assets attributable to speed.

Speed training is sometimes dreaded by players because it often takes the form of shuttles, which involves repetition runs over short distances.

If you are on your own you can race against the clock, but the presence of a partner always adds spice and that

SOCCER

competitive element.

You can use some of the suggested routines or use your imagination and think up some of your own, but try to make them realistic to game situations. Distance should range from a minimum of 5–6yd (approx. 5m) to a maximum 30yd (27m). It must also involve turns and changes of direction.

The strengthening of legs and upper body will greatly assist your performance; both arms and legs should act like pumps. To illustrate this, try sprinting on the spot, bend your head forward, tuck your elbows in and for 30-second bursts, pump your arms and knees up and down in short sharp movements, and take short strides rather than long ones.

That concludes our look at fitness – don't shun this aspect of soccer. Just because you have the basic skills required to play the game does not mean you are geared up to becoming a top class player. Skills are no good without fitness, just as fitness is no good without the basic skills. You need both.

Go out and enjoy your training. After a while, when you can see your benefits from it, then you will start to enjoy the rigours of training.

EIGHT

INJURIES
PREVENTION AND CURE

No matter how hard a player trains and prepares himself for 90 minutes of football, he will at some time suffer some form of injury. It can take the form of a strain or pull which stops him playing for a couple of weeks, or something more serious like a broken leg, which can take up to a year to heal. In some cases the injury can be so severe that it ends a promising career. Brian Clough's playing career was ended prematurely due to a knee injury. More recently players such as Kevin Beattie (Ipswich Town) and Danny Thomas (Tottenham Hotspur) have seen promising careers shattered because of injury.

The fact that football is competitive and a contact sport means there is a greater risk of injury. Obviously that risk can be reduced by a player training regularly and strengthening his body to withstand the tackles and physical contact. Stretching and warming up before you play or train will reduce the risk of pulled or strained muscles, which are often caused by using them cold in a game.

Players can protect themselves by wearing shinpads and ankle protectors. Goalkeepers have elbow protectors in their shirts and thigh protectors in their shorts. Some players don't wear shinpads, but if they reduce the risk of injury, they have to be a good thing and should really be worn.

Finally, an area of injury prevention which is rarely considered is the development of skill and skilful play.

Showing a player dribbling techniques and how to avoid reckless and lunging tackles, and coaching goalkeepers on diving techniques, especially at the feet of forwards, will all help to reduce the chances of injuries. It is certainly a point worth considering when encouraging good skilful play.

However, accepting that you will be injured at some time, let's look at the type of injuries you are likely to receive, and how to treat them.

The most common injuries are cuts, bruises and minor strains, which can often be dealt with by the player himself.

Cuts

Provided it is not a deep wound, ensure that it is cleaned with an antiseptic cream and protected with a plaster or bandage.

Minor sprains and bruises

The treatment of sprains and bruises can be remembered by the *acronym* RICE.

R for rest: You must stop playing or using the injured part of your body, or you could worsen the injury or cause permanent damage.

SOCCER

I for ice: Applying ice to the injured area will reduce the swelling. Do not apply ice directly onto the skin, but place the ice cubes in a plastic bag, wrap in a damp cloth and then place them on the injured area.

C for compression: Wrap a bandage firmly, but not tightly around the area and apply ice.

E for elevation: Try and lift the injured part above the height of the heart *i.e.* for a knee injury you should lay down resting your leg on a small stool.

Quick application of the above treatment will reduce the amount of time you will be out of action.

Recovery can be helped further with heat treatment. The use of a heat lamp, hot water bottle or deep heat creams for short periods (10/15min) will help the healing process.

Footballers receive many different injuries, from simple bruises to serious breaks. Listed below are some of the injuries which regularly cause players to miss games.

Ankles

Injuries: Most commonly, sprains and tears of the ligaments surrounding the ankle.
Treatment : Initially 'RICE'. Keep your body weight off the ankle, and carry out mobility exercises to strengthen the muscles around the ankle. Ensure that boots offer adequate ankle support.

Achilles Tendon

Located at the rear of the ankle, between the heel bone and calf muscles.
Injuries: Strain (can be painful when kicked), tear, or worse a complete break.
Treatment: To reduce the swelling apply 'RICE'. Strains will require rest however, and a tear will require surgery.

Knees

There are four ligaments located around the knee with cartilage on the inside of the knee and on the outside.
Injuries: Tears and strains to the ligaments and torn or worn cartilage.
Treatment: Strains require rest, while a torn ligament will need surgery. Damaged cartilage will require removal through surgery.

Hamstrings

Hamstrings are the tendons at the back of the upper leg between the lower back and the knee.
Injuries: Tearing of fibres, and either pulls or strains.
Treatment: Initially 'RICE'. Then rest. Ease your way back with gentle stretching exercises.

Groin

The muscles between the pelvis and thigh.
Injuries: Strains or tears.
Treatment: Rest, heat treatment, and gentle stretching exercises.

The above information is to help and guide you with your injuries. There is no substitute for expert medical advice.

It is also useful for players to carry some medical items of their own, such as plasters, bandages, antiseptic cream, cotton wool and pain relieving spray. It is amazing how many amateur clubs do not carry the basic medical equipment, so it is always handy to have your own personal stock.

It is possible to have a sporting career without a single injury, but usually the stress, strain and pressure on the body will, at some time, take its toll. So be prepared.

NINE

PROFESSIONAL STYLE

The skills and techniques highlighted throughout the book can be seen being performed at football matches all over Britain during the football season.

Sadly we do not have too many opportunities to watch the top continentals perform live. However, the increased coverage by television allows us the opportunity to watch action by top players.

Let's take a close look at some of the game's outstanding players and look at some of the skills which make them outstanding.

The British game as always has been renowned for producing top class goalkeepers and at 40 years of age Peter Shilton can be classed as the elder statesman of the British game, but at the same time he retains his youthful enthusiasm for the game. A perfectionist, he still works and trains hard on all aspects of his game and typifies how hard work can get you to the top. A feature of his game, apart from his obvious ability, is his constant talking to the players in front of him, encouraging and passing on information.

Everton's Neville Southall is regarded as one of the top goalkeepers in Europe, and possibly the world. It should be an encouragement to all youngsters that he was spotted playing non-league football, and worked his way through the lower divisions before arriving at Goodison Park. He dominates the penalty area and his excellent positional play makes shot-stopping look easy.

The move that brought Jim Leighton from Aberdeen to Manchester United was recognition of his many years of safe and consistent goalkeeping north of the border. His two strengths lie in his excellent handling and superb positional play. When talking about goalkeepers, you cannot ignore Liverpool's Zimbabwe-born Bruce Grobbelaar. Always one for the spectacular, hence his nick name 'The Clown', his handling techniques and the ability to cope with crosses with apparent ease are major features of Bruce's game.

Defenders come in many shapes and sizes and so do their styles and techniques.

England's Terry Butcher is a big strong centre back who dominates in the air and is strong in the tackle. This game is all about preventing the opposition from scoring. In contrast Liverpool's Alan Hansen is regarded as a more elegant player who tends to dominate by using his ability to anticipate situations and quickly switch defence to attack.

The European teams are better known for producing 'footballing' defenders and the Dutch national side uses Ronald Koemand and Frank Rijkard. They are both good defenders, but are at their most

SOCCER

dangerous when running the ball out of defence.

Two other defenders to make note of are Nottingham Forest's Des Walker and Queen's Park Rangers' Gary Parker. They are good examples of defenders who quickly anticipate what is happening around them and both have the ability to break out quickly from defence.

The midfield area provides us with so many different contrasts in styles with some players having particular strengths and others having good all-round ability.

England and Manchester United captain Bryan Robson is probably the best example of an all-round midfielder. He is strong, has the ability to win the ball, is a good passer, has tremendous work rate, and has that priceless ability of popping up in the opposition's penalty box and scoring goals. In addition, he has the talent of being a great leader.

In players like John Barnes and Chris Waddle we look at midfielders with similar strengths, but different from those of Bryan Robson. Both Barnes and Waddle are at their best when running at defenders, and both possess good dribbling skills and excellent pace. Both have different running styles but have good balance and are very comfortable on the ball. Another feature of their game is their ability to cross the ball with deadly accuracy and quality.

Again we can look to the continent to see the greatest exponents of this particular style with Dutch captain Ruud Gullit and Argentina's captain Diego Maradona being classic examples of outstanding midfield players.

Both specialise in the attacking aspect of midfield play. Gullit is very quick and deceptive for a tall man, and after going past a defender is a deadly striker of the ball. His height gives him a distinctive advantage in the air.

Maradona is also at his best when running at players. He has brilliant close-ball control and a full repertoire of tricks and turns which he is not frightened to use. Although both Gullit and Maradona are best remembered for their many goals, it should not be forgotten that they are also good passers of the ball and have the vision required to exploit defensive errors.

The British game has players emerging with similar qualities; Tottenham's Paul Gascoigne, Arsenal's David Rocastle and Celtic's Paul McStay are among possible British contenders for comparison with Gullit and Maradona.

And finally, to the game's great strikers. Britain has a reputation for producing some marvellous strikers, and the list of foreign clubs who have signed British speaks volumes for the quality of the British game.

All strikers have that inbuilt quality of 'being in the right place at the right time'. But that is coupled with a lot of hard work and understanding. Although the end product is the same – a goal – strikers have their own style and methods.

Welsh striker Ian Rush is so quick to react to situations in the penalty area that he has the ball in the back of the net before a defender can respond. A large proportion of his goals are scored with an instinctive reaction.

England's top striker Gary Lineker relies upon good timing for a lot of his goals. You will see him arriving in the penalty box usually to strike the ball first time. If you watch him he will do a lot of running off the ball losing his marker, and popping up in the box unmarked.

Like Rush, Lineker has good speed off the mark and both players prowl across the defensive line and quickly pounce and punish any lapse in concentration.

Nottingham Forest's Des Walker's good timing allows him to rise above the other players to make a good clearing header.

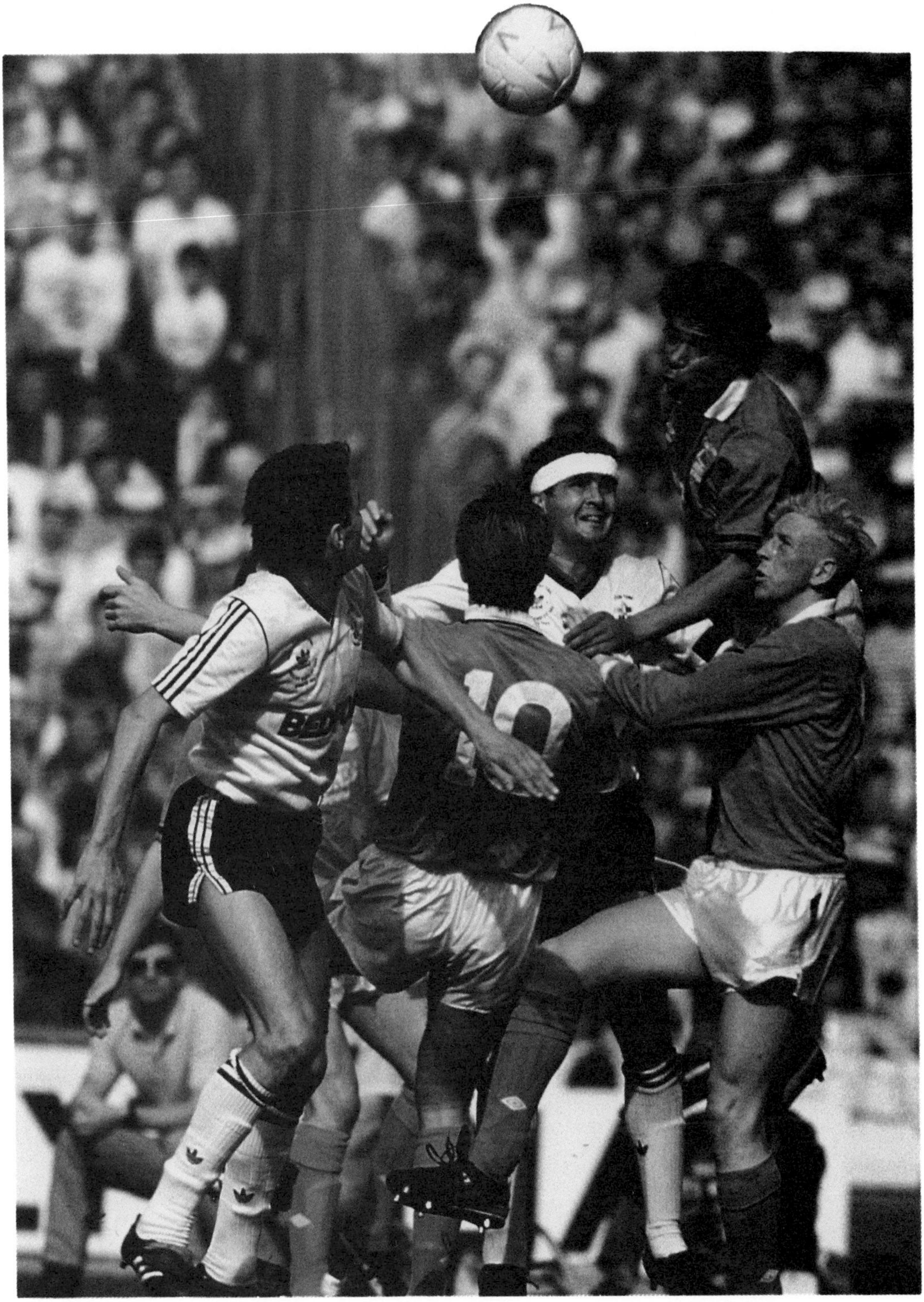

SOCCER

Welsh international striker Mark Hughes has a different style. He is a strong rugged player who does a lot of work outside the box. He is very difficult to knock off the ball and is particularly dangerous with shots on the turn. His ability to hit shots on the volley should be an inspiration and example to all aspiring strikers.

Scotland's Maurice (Mo) Johnston adopts a different style again. He is prepared to take players on in and around the box in order to create an opening. This often produces the spectacular in terms of dribbles and shots. This type of striker has the added bonus of often winning penalties, because he commits defenders with his dribbling skills.

Strikers, like defenders, come in a variety of shapes and sizes. Scotland's Graeme Sharp and England's Mark Hateley are both big and strong, and a larger percentage of their goals are headed because they thrive on crosses and balls in the air.

Although many of our strikers have been sought after by European teams, there are still many European-bred strikers worth looking at.

Dutch international Marco van Basten has a ferocious shot and is prepared to shoot from any angle. Denmark's Michael Laudrup combines lightning pace with dribbling skills to score his goals. And finally for improvisation, there is Real Madrid's athletic Hugo Sanchez, the man renowned for his overhead bicycle kicks.

We have highlighted just a few of the players whom you can see displaying the techniques and skills we have made you aware of. Watch how the top players combine those skills. You will learn from them. When you feel confident, try and use them in a game, and don't be put off if it doesn't work first time or every time.

Finally it is important that you play the game in the right spirit and you adopt high standards of behaviour and sportsmanship.

Great emphasis is put on winning, but what is most important is that you enjoy your involvement in the game.

It doesn't matter if it's the local park match or the World Cup Final, there is nothing more enjoyable for the players, and those watching, than good techniques and skilful football played in the right spirit of mind.

TESTING TIME

A series of questions to see how much you have learned on the foregoing pages.

1. Which are the three main areas of the body which need to be developed when controlling the ball?
   (a) head–feet–chest
   (b) feet–thighs–chest
   (c) thighs–chest–head

2. Which of these is important when controlling the ball?
   (a) move into the line of the ball
   (b) have your back to the opponent's goal
   (c) have your head up and ready to see where you are going to pass

3. What is the biggest problem in controlling the ball with your thigh?
   (a) taking your eye off the ball
   (b) moving the thigh upwards as it meets the ball
   (c) trying to control the ball while on the move

4. How will breathing out at impact when controlling the ball on your chest help?
   (a) It will help you to relax
   (b) It will put you in the 'ready' position to make a run with the ball after you have controlled it
   (c) It will create a hollow area on your chest for the ball to make contact with

5. What is the name of the defensive system in which defenders cover a specific area of the pitch and mark any attacker who comes into it?
   (a) blanket defence
   (b) zonal defence
   (c) overall defence

6. ... and what name is given to the type of defensive system where a defender is assigned a specific player to mark throughout the match?
   (a) Single-man marking
   (b) Solo-defence
   (c) Man-to-man marking

7. What should the *first* thought of a defender be?
   (a) Can I intercept?
   (b) If I tackle the opposing player will I win the ball?
   (c) Am I likely to give away a foul if I make the tackle?

8. Which of the following are all attributes of good tackling?
   (a) keeping your eye on the ball
   (b) not rushing the tackle
   (c) good stance

SOCCER

9. What is the golden rule of defending?
   (a) Tackle at an early stage of the game to let the opponents know your capabilities
   (b) Read the game
   (c) Stay on your feet whenever possible

10. The following are all important features when covering, but which one would you say is the most important?
    (a) Setting the correct body angle in relation to the first defender
    (b) Not being too close to the first defender
    (c) Keeping your eye on the ball, not your first defender

11. Which one word is missing from the following three statements all to do with defending?
    (a) Aim to ...... the ball as high as possible
    (b) Make sure you get distance when you ...... the ball
    (c) Try to ...... the ball towards the touchlines

12. What is the first priority of a midfield player?
    (a) attacking
    (b) defending
    (c) creating openings

13. Which one of the following is NOT one of the two basic principles of running with the ball?
    (a) Cover the ground as quickly as possible
    (b) Keep the ball close to your feet
    (c) Make as few touches of the ball as possible

14. What are the two ways of dribbling past a defender?

15. Which type of pass is designed to go over defenders' heads?
    (a) the straight pass
    (b) the swerving pass
    (c) the lofted pass

16. When making a lofted pass should your upper body be slightly leaning:
    (a) forwards
    (b) backwards
    (c) to the side

17. When heading, which part of the ball should your forehead make contact with in order to gain maximum height?
    (a) the middle of the ball
    (b) the bottom half of the ball
    (c) the top half of the ball

18. When bending or swerving the ball is it done with:
    (a) the inside of the foot
    (b) the outside of the foot
    (c) either

19. Which shots are the most awkward for goalkeepers?
    (a) Those hit towards the bottom corners of the goal
    (b) Those hit towards the top corners of the goal
    (c) Those hit about chest-height

20. As an attacker, how would you get more power into a header?
    (a) By running to the ball and meeting it while moving forward
    (b) Making contact with the ball at its highest point
    (c) Correct balance

21. What is regarded as the most common, and safest, way a goalkeeper should deal with ground shots?
    (a) the spread technique
    (b) the stooping technique
    (c) the kneeling technique

QUESTIONS

22. When punching the ball should the goalkeeper use:
    (a) the fist nearest to the ball
    or
    (b) both fists

23. Which type of kick should a goalkeeper employ if he has two big strikers as target men?
    (a) volley kick
    (b) half-volley kick

24. What percentage of all goals are scored from set plays?
    (a) 10%
    (b) 20%
    (c) 30%
    (d) 40%

ANSWERS

1. **(b)** feet–thighs–chest
2. **(a)** move into the line of the ball
3. **(b)** the thigh is moving upwards as it meets the ball
4. **(c)** It will create a hollow area on your chest for the ball to make contact with
5. **(b)** zonal defence
6. **(c)** Man-to-man marking
7. **(a)** Can I intercept?
8. All three are important
9. While all three are important aspects of successful defending, the golden rule is **(c)** Stay on your feet whenever possible. So, if you are going to make a tackle, be confident of winning the ball.
10. **(b)** Not being too close to the first defender. If you are, then the attacker could beat both of you at the same time, thus rendering the cover useless.
11. Head
12. **(b)** defending
13. **(b)** Keep the ball close to your feet
14. (1) Forcing him to go the wrong way by playing a 'trick' or dummy
    (2) By a change of pace, thus enabling you to push the ball past him
15. **(c)** the lofted pass.
16. **(b)** backwards
17. **(b)** the bottom half of the ball
18. **(c)** either
19. **(a)** Those hit towards the bottom corners of the goal
20. **(a)** By running to the ball and meeting it while moving forward
21. **(c)** the kneeling technique
22. **(b)** both fists
23. **(a)** volley kick
24. **(d)** 40%

INDEX

Page references in **bold** refer to illustrations and captions.

Achilles tendon injury 120
arms, exercises for 104–5

ball control 8–16
  with chest 14–16
  with feet 9–12
  with thigh 12–14
Barnes, John **7,** 36, 122
Beardsley, Peter 24
Beckenbauer, Franz 18
Butcher, Terry 121

calf, exercises for 103
catching 76–9
chest, ball control with 14–16
corners 95–9
  inswinging 97
  outswinging 98–1
covering 25–6
crosses
  dealing with 74–81
  scoring from 61
Cruyff, Johan 51, **115**

Dalglish, Kenny **2**
defensive play 17–30, 31
defensive systems 17
defensive wall 92–4
  beating 86–92
distributing the ball (goalkeeper) 81–5
diving header 61
diving saves 69–72
dribbling 36–7

feet, ball control with 9–12
  ball in air 11
  ball on ground 10
  under pressure 11
feint 37, 51
fitness training 102–18
flexibility, training for 102–5
free kicks 86–94

Gascoigne, Paul 122
goal scoring 47, 54–64
goalkeeping 65–85
  catching 76–9
  and corners 95, 97
  crosses, dealing with 74–81
  and defensive wall 94
  deflecting 81
  diving 69–72
  handling 65–9
  kicking 81–2

kneeling 65–8
positioning 72–4
punching 80–1
stance 65
stooping 68
throwing 82–3
Grobbelaar, Bruce 65, 81, 121
groin
  exercises for 103
  injuries to 120
Gullit, Ruud **62,** 122

hamstrings
  exercises for 103
  injuries to 120
Hansen, Alan 18, 121
Hartford, Mick 58
Hateley, Mark 58, 124
  heading 58
  defensive 27–30
  diving headers 61
  goal scoring 58–64
Hughes, Mark 51, 58, **84,** 124

injuries 119–20
intercepting 18

Johnston, Mo 124

kneeling technique 68
Koemand, Ronald 121

Laudrup, Michael 124
legs
  exercises for 103–4, 108–9
  injuries to 120
Leighton, Jim 65, 121
Lineker, Gary **28,** 40, 64, 122

McMahon, Steve **107**
McStay, Paul **22,** 122
man-to-man marking 17
Maradona, Diego 36, **50,** 122
medical equipment 120
middle body, exercises for 104
midfield play 31–46
  dribbling 36–7
  passing 40–6
  running with the ball 32–6
Moore, Bobby 18

Parker, Gary 122
passes, making 33–5, 40–6
  bending 42–5
  lofted 40–2

straight 45
swerving 42, 45
passes, receiving 33
protective wear 119
punching 80–1

Rijkaard, Frank **111,** 121
Robson, Bryan 87, **106,** 122
Rocastle, David **44,** 122
running 107–8
running with the ball 32–6
Rush, Ian 40, 101, 122

Sanchez, Hugo 58, **93,** 124
'scissors' 38
set plays 86–101
Sharp, Graeme 124
Shilton, Peter 65, **66,** 69, 121
shooting 54–64
  half-volley 56–8
  heading 58–64
shoulders, exercises for 104–5
sit ups 110
skipping 108
Southall, Neville 65, 69, **73,** 121
speed, exercises for 117–8
sprains 119–20
squat thrusts 109
stamina, exercises for 107–8
step-ups 108
strength, exercises for 108–17
stride jumps 109
strikers 47–64
  beating defenders 47–51
  heading 58–64
  receiving the ball 47–51
  scoring 54–64
sweeper 17

tackling 19–24
  block 19–21
  sliding 23–4
thigh, ball control with 12–14
throwing 82–3
throw-ins 99

Van Basten, Marco **34,** 124

Waddle, Chris 33, 36, **57,** 122
Walker, Des 122, **123**
Webb, Neil **15**